# CASTLES OF BRITAIN

## PATRICK CORMACK

ABOVE The dramatic silhouette of the Norman keep at Rochester Castle, Kent
OVERLEAF Eilean Donan Castle, Highlands, on its island site at the head of Loch Alsh

# CASTLES

# OF BRITAIN

PATRICK CORMACK

CRESCENT BOOKS
New York

# CONTENTS

*To Charles and Richard*

AUTHOR'S ACKNOWLEDGMENTS

In addition to thanking all those who have provided the many excellent illustrations for this book, I would like to extend my thanks to Wendy Dallas, of Weidenfeld & Nicolson, for her help in choosing the illustrations and for her general patience; Ian Stanley for helping to chase and collect vast quantities of literature for my perusal; and, above all, to my wife who did most of the typing, much of the time working to what seemed an impossibly tight timetable.

PATRICK CORMACK
Chelsea, 1982

Copyright © 1982 Patrick Cormack

This 1982 edition published by Crescent Books, distributed by Crown Publishers, Inc.

Originally published in Great Britain in 1982 by Artus Publishing Company Limited, 91 Clapham High Street, London SW4 7TA, England

Designed by Allison Waterhouse

Library of Congress Cataloging in Publication Data

Cormack, Patrick, 1939–
    Castles of Britain.
    1. Castles – Great Britain – Guide-books.
    2. Great Britain – History, Local.
    3. Architecture – Great Britain.
    I. Title.
DA660.C63   1982      914.1      82–5110
ISBN 0–517–27544–9          AACR2

h g f e d c b a

Typeset in England by Keyspools, Golborne, Lancashire

Colour separations by Newsele Litho

Printed and bound in Italy by LEGO, Vicenza

Loch Long

■ EILEEN DONAN
Loch Duich
Loch Alsh

Aberdeen •

CRATHES ■

• Glasgow   ■ EDINBURGH

• York

• Manchester

Menai Strait

• Newcastle

■ CAERNAEVON

Severn

• Birmingham

STOKESAY ■   ■ LUDLOW   ■ KENILWORTH

Wye   Teme

Usk

■ GOODRICH

■ RAGLAN

CAERPHILLY ■   ■ BERKELEY

CASTELL ■   • Cardiff   • Bristol
COCH

Tower of
London

■ WINDSOR

Thames

Medway   ■ ROCHESTER

Lea   ■ DEAL

HEVER ■   ■ LEEDS

■ OLD SARUM   Arun   Rother   ■ DOVER

ARUNDEL ■   ■ BODIAM

■ TINTAGEL   ■ MAIDEN

English Channel

• Plymouth

PENDENNIS ■
Carrick
Roads

# INTRODUCTION

CASTLES have always fascinated me. I first knew real excitement when I struggled to climb the observation tower at Lincoln Castle and imagined firing arrows into the enemy camp below. That was the earliest memory that came to me when I began work on this book. But there were many others. I remembered a clear spring morning at Arundel, in Sussex, when the daffodils brightened the stone and the only sound was of the Earl Marshal's standard stirring in the breeze. I remembered the day I first discovered Goodrich, in Hereford and Worcester, and looked down, as its first defenders must have done, on the sparkling ribbon of the Wye beneath ; and a September evening when my wife and I were the last pre-dusk visitors to Castle Urquhart, the fortified promontory on Loch Ness which for so long controlled the passage from the Western Highlands. And I remembered a frost-sharp November night when the cold gave an added ring to the challenge and response at the Ceremony of the Keys in the Tower of London.

It is no wonder that castles, and especially ruined castles, have had such a strong romantic hold on the imaginations of poets, novelists and artists. This hold was never more simply or better expressed than by an anonymous Anglo-Saxon poet writing in those dark years of the ninth century :

> The place where multitudes of men breath'd joy and woe
> Long ago has crumbled.

It is something of a paradox that buildings which evoke such powerful nostalgia were erected for such unpeaceful purposes and witnessed so many scenes of violence and brutality. But much of their charm lies in their desolation. They are, and yet they have ceased to be : in them our powers of imagination are set to work. Those powers can best operate, however, on the basis of some knowledge, and that is what this book seeks to provide for those who are fascinated by castles but have yet to study them.

The earliest defences erected in Britain were Bronze Age and Iron Age hillforts built a thousand years or more before Christ : there are some two and a half thousand of these on the mainland alone. Many of them were very small, mere defended farms and homesteads, and are now barely discernible even to the trained eye, but at Maiden Castle in Dorset we can see some of the most extensive and impressive earthwork fortifications in Europe.

The extraordinary brochs of northern Scotland and the Isles date from around the same period. Gurness Broch in Orkney, for instance, was built some two thousand years ago of unmortared stone and yet its defences still stand to a height of 13 metres (40 feet), and its double walls testify not only to the fear in which the inhabitants lived, but also to their remarkable facility for building effectively daunting fortifications.

Traces of Roman forts are disappointingly few. At Porchester in Hampshire there are remnants of Roman walls, as there are at Colchester in Essex, at Lincoln, and at Burgh Castle in Suffolk, and there is a superb

Roman survival at Caerleon in Gwent. But by far the most famous and extensive Roman fortification is Hadrian's Wall and the fort on the wall at Housesteads in Northumberland gives a particularly clear idea of Roman military architecture.

Little evidence remains of the fortresses of the Anglo-Saxons, although we know from the Anglo-Saxon Chronicle that as early as 547 the Saxons fortified Bamburgh in Northumberland. Tintagel in Cornwall was refortified during the Anglo-Saxon period, though most of the existing ruin dates from Norman times. Precisely what the Saxons did and how they did it remains a subject of scholarly conjecture and debate. What is certain is that Alfred and his successors erected fortifications that were effective both as defensive positions and as strongholds from which to control the countryside.

We leave the realm of conjecture and enter the first real period of castle building with the Norman Conquest. In order to subdue, control and command his new territory, William of Normandy erected a series of castles throughout England. Most were initially built of earth, but by the middle of the twelfth century most of these early earthwork structures had been replaced by stone castles. We can see fine examples of Norman work at Rochester in Kent and at Ludlow in Shropshire, at the Tower of London, at Castle Hedingham in Essex, at Lewes in Sussex, at Durham and Lincoln, and at Richmond in Yorkshire.

Under the Normans and their Plantagenet successors, the castle dominated both the landscapes and the people. Henry II, his sons Richard I and John, and his grandson Henry III, were all great castle builders and examples of their work can be seen at Conisbrough and Middleham in Yorkshire and at Framlingham in Suffolk.

Castle building in Britain reached its splendid climax in the thirteenth century in Wales. De Clare's Caerphilly in Gwent was the first of the concentric castles and, covering 12 hectares (30 acres), it remains the biggest castle in Wales. It was followed by the royal castles of Conway, Beaumaris and Caernarvon, all in Gwynedd, the last two built on either side of the Menai Straits to symbolize Edward I's power in his Welsh dominions.

As society became less turbulent, and the need for strong defences was replaced by the desire for comfort and the wish to settle in a fixed abode, so the castle gradually evolved into the fortified country house. We see the beginning of this process at Hever, Leeds and Penshurst, all in Kent, at Bodiam in Sussex and, on a smaller scale, at Stokesay, that enchantingly domestic fortified manor house in Shropshire.

Not that the age of castle building was absolutely at an end. In the sixteenth century Henry VIII built a series of coastal defences which rank among the most interesting of our castles, the best example of which is Deal in Kent, although Pendennis in Cornwall saw more action, not only in the sixteenth century but also during the Civil War. It was during that war between Charles I and his Parliament, as Royalist stronghold after stronghold fell and castles were slighted to prevent their being of further military use, that the age of the castle came to an end. The last castle to surrender in the Civil War was Raglan in Gwent and its capitulation set the seal on the Royalist defeat.

In Scotland, castles still had a final part to play in domestic strife during the Jacobite uprisings. Edinburgh itself, for instance, held out even when the Young Pretender and his forces took the city in 1745.

In England and in Scotland a number of castles have remained in continuous occupation, sometimes, as at Berkeley in Gloucestershire and Alnwick in Northumberland, by the same family through many centuries. In spite of possessing comfortable domestic quarters these castles still have all the appearance of fortresses, generally because of the great romantic interest in castles which persisted from the end of the eighteenth century until well into the nineteenth. This was the time when a number of castles – Arundel and Alnwick, for example – received the attentions of architects such as Wyatt and Salvin to re-establish their original martial appearance. Many of the nineteenth-century 'castles' were either virtually or entirely new creations. Windsor was almost completely rebuilt, as was Belvoir in Leicestershire, and even in the remotest corners of the land country gentlemen exercised their medieval fantasies. At Penrhyn in Gwynedd a Welsh slate millionaire created a mighty fortress, and at Tealby in the Lincolnshire Wolds Tennyson's grandfather built a castle complete with portcullis, drawbridge and jousting ground.

This book attempts to guide the reader through these various phases in Britain's castle building. By taking representative examples of differing types of castle, I hope to provide not only interesting information about the buildings selected but an idea of how to enjoy others in greater measure. It has been very difficult to choose just twenty-five and those readers whose particular favourites have been omitted will, I hope, be forgiving. A real attempt has been made to achieve a geographical and historical balance, and historical accuracy too, although it must be stressed that there is still much scholarly disagreement over our earlier fortifications, as for instance over the precise origin of the motte-and-bailey castle : even in recent years long accepted notions have been upset by archaeological discoveries. All a book like this can hope to do is to base its conclusions on the latest generally accepted evidence.

One final word. Many castles have been constantly altered through the centuries and it would be possible to put some, like Tintagel or Windsor, in one of several chapters. I hope that the divisions that have been made will not seem too arbitrary.

# 1 BEFORE

The first military posts to be built in Britain were the hillforts of the late Stone, Bronze and Iron Ages. Some of them date from before 2000 BC and almost two thousand five hundred of them have been identified and are marked on the Six-Inch Ordnance Survey maps. The largest were in effect garrison towns of a very primitive nature, but the smallest – and most of them were very small indeed – were little more than family stockades in which a group of peasants would take refuge with their stocks and herds at the approach of danger. The earliest of these hillforts were very simple earthworks defended by a single rampart, but those built in the two centuries or so before the Romans came were of a much more sophisticated design, with a series of linear earthworks. We can see examples of the smaller type, direct ancestors of the fortified manor houses of the Middle Ages, at Little Woodberry in Wiltshire and Staple Howe in Yorkshire. But the most spectacular of all the hillforts is Maiden Castle in Dorset. It had its origins long before the Iron Age and we shall look at it in detail later. There are other hillforts of similar construction at Hambledon, Hodd Hill and Eggardon, all in Dorset, at Bredon in Shropshire and at Barbury in Wiltshire. Some of them were enormous : Binden Hill in Dorset and Hengistbury Head in Hampshire each cover over 80 hectares (200 acres).

From such a garrison the tribal chief ruled his district. Contained within the ramparts were the domestic buildings and the temples, though generally public buildings were outside the fortifications, as were the tribal burial grounds. From what is left of these forts it is difficult to be precise about methods of construction or even their exact purpose. Many consisted of one particularly high earthwork rampart with two or more lower ones in front, each having a steep sloping inner face which would deprive an attacker of cover. These ramparts were timber strengthened, but this rendered them vulnerable to assault by fire and many appear to have been overcome in this way. The entrance was always a particularly weak point and there were many and various attempts to give added protection by using large quantities of timber and, later, stone. The Celtic Britons who built these forts had to rely very heavily on antler picks and shovels made from the shoulder blades of oxen. Maiden Castle itself was reworked and improved several times over a period of a thousand years or so before it was finally stormed and taken by the Romans. Although they were used as bastions against Roman might, few of these forts were built to withstand a long siege and indeed most did not have a water supply within them. They were of small use against a well-armed, well-drilled and determined attacker.

The Romans themselves needed defended camps and bases from which to subdue, and later to rule,

opposite Spanning the north of England from west to east is Hadrian's Wall, guarded by sixteen forts. The most spectacular of them is Housesteads in Northumberland, which has been fully excavated and gives a clear idea of a Roman fortification.

# THE NORMANS

ABOVE The magnificent amphitheatre outside the walls of the Second Augustine Legion's headquarters at Caerleon-on-Usk, in Gwent.

their most northerly province. It was not very inviting territory. From the remaining wild areas in the Highlands of Scotland, the Welsh mountains, the Yorkshire moors and the more desolate parts of the south-west, we can get some idea of the difficulty of the terrain the Romans found. There were no true roads before they came, only trodden tracks that were completely impassable in winter. About two-thirds of the country was covered by thick forest in which wolves and wild boars ranged freely. Much of the remaining third, in areas around Romsey in Hampshire, Glastonbury in Somerset and Crowland in Lincolnshire for example, was marsh and bogland.

It is surprising that more of the earthworks they subdued were not used by the Romans as the basis of their own first fortifications. At some places, such as Hodd Hill, they did build a new fort within the ramparts of the old, but for the most part they established their own new towns and fortified them, and by the end of the first century after Christ almost all of the old British hillforts had been deserted.

Partly because of the havoc caused by the invaders who came when the legions withdrew, and partly because many Romano-British towns have been engulfed in subsequent urban development, there are not many traces left of Roman fortifications. Romans built towns rather than castles. Their power was preserved in the legions that went forth to conquer ; thus the products of Roman military architecture were essentially bases that were themselves a transformation into stone of the defensive stockades which the legions first created when they captured any hostile territory. York and Chester were stone

LEFT Porchester Castle in Hampshire formed part of the coastal defences erected by the Romans against attack from the Continent. The perimeter wall and fourteen of the original semi-circular towers still stand to a height of 6 metres (20 feet). In the foreground is the huge square keep built by Henry I in the twelfth century.

versions of such camps, rectangular in design and with regular street patterns that facilitated the rapid assembly of large bodies of soldiers.

At Colchester, built towards the end of the first century, we can still see the Roman West Gate, and at Lincoln the Newport Arch (although that, alas, is a recent reconstruction following the demolition of the original arch by a fish lorry); at Caerleon-on-Usk, which was romantically woven into Arthurian legend, were the headquarters of the Second Augustine Legion. Significant areas of this 20-hectare (50-acre) site have been excavated, revealing traces of a wall which was reinforced with turrets at regular intervals of 46 metres (50 yards). The most interesting feature at Caerleon is the amphitheatre, excavated some fifty years ago and once known as King Arthur's Round Table. Almost every legionary fortress town would have had such a theatre, which would have doubled as a parade ground.

Policing a vast empire with long and tenuous supply lines was never easy, and the Romans wherever possible used fixed lines of defence, the most famous of which is Hadrian's Wall, built in the early second century and spanning a distance of 117·5 kilometres (73 miles) from Carlisle to Newcastle. There are sixteen forts along the wall, at 6·5-kilometre (4-mile) intervals, and at every Roman mile is a Mile Castle. Housesteads Fort has been fully excavated and gives us a clear idea of a legionaire's post. The purpose of the Wall was to deter potential aggressors and stop border raids. It could not have withstood a mass attack but would have given time for the troops to be mustered, and was linked by a semaphore system to the main northern garrison in York. Some years after it was completed, in about 140 AD, Antoninus Pius had the Antonine Wall built to the north. This was a shorter and altogether less impressive affair and was maintained as an advance line for only half a century.

We also have significant remains of the coastal defences which the Romans erected under a senior general – known as the Count of the Saxon Shore – to repel seaborne invaders from the Continent. There are remains of this highly sophisticated system at Burgh in Suffolk, Bradwell in Essex, Reculver in Kent, and Pevensey in Sussex. By far the most impressive, however, are at Porchester in Hampshire. There the walls still stand to a height of 6 metres (20 feet), flint bonded with brick and slate and 3 metres (10 feet) thick. Fourteen of the original towers around the wall are still in good repair.

As the Romans, under attack even in the heart of their Empire, withdrew from their northern frontiers, their defences fell, often without a struggle, to the new invaders from northern Europe. In an

LEFT Offa's Dyke at Springhill, near Clun in Shropshire, built by the Anglo-Saxons to defend the border between England and Wales.

endeavour to hold fast, the native British re-used some of the old hillforts and even built new ones, but in vain.

The Angles and Saxons had their own military system. The most famous of their structures is the 193-kilometre (120-mile) Offa's Dyke, the rampart and ditch which marked the western border of Mercia with Wales. Most of their dykes have totally disappeared but there is a 13-kilometre (8-mile) stretch in Cambridgeshire known as Devil's Dyke. We know little of the fortifications of the Anglo-Saxons. Almost certainly they re-occupied and re-used a number of Roman bases such as Colchester, but the fact that these forest dwellers quite naturally used so much wood meant that not enough of their buildings have survived to give us a clear idea of their defences, even though we know from the *Anglo-Saxon Chronicle* that the bases built by Alfred the Great played a significant part in his defeat of the Danes. His successors continued his work: among the fortified towns that they built were Bridgnorth, Stafford, Tamworth and Warwick in the Midlands, and Hertford, Buckingham, Bedford and Stamford, and they rebuilt the Roman walls at Bath, Winchester, Porchester, Exeter and Chester. But because they used mainly wood and because later generations built on the same sites, we have to rely for our knowledge on documentary rather than archaeological evidence.

Tintagel, in Cornwall, the most romantic castle of the pre-Norman Conquest period, belongs to myth and legend, that misty land between fantasy and history peopled by Arthur and his knights. Although most of the Arthurian stories were the creation of Geoffrey of Monmouth in the twelfth century and Malory in the fifteenth, there is no doubt that the British did offer a long resistance when the Romans had gone. Led by shadowy figures, sometimes of royal lineage, they fought against the invading Saxons. Around 470 AD Aurelius Ambrosianus held out in the Glastonbury region, and after him came Arthur. At some time between 490 and 516 a British victory was won at a place called Mount Badon. We do not know where that was but what we do know is that the leader was a Christian hero known in the Welsh Marches, no later than the ninth century, as 'Arthur of Britain'. This was the warrior king who was to become the saint of chivalry all over Europe, and whose story and legend merged together and are forever associated with the romantically mysterious Tintagel.

# MAIDEN CASTLE

## DORSET

MAIDEN CASTLE IN DORSET is the most famous of the ancient hilltop fortifications in the south of England. First established in about 3000 BC it was adopted and adapted over the centuries until it fell to the Romans in 44 AD. Though it was reoccupied by the Saxons (until finally deserted in the fifth century), Maiden Castle is today the most evocative reminder of those years before the Roman conquerors came from Gaul to the misty, tree-clad island across the sea.

There is no better description of Maiden than that of Dorset's greatest writer, Thomas Hardy:

At every step forward it rises higher against the south sky, with an obtrusive personality which compels the senses to regard it and consider . . . The profile of the whole stupendous ruin, as seen at a distance of a mile eastwards, is as clearly cut as that of a marble inlay. It is varied with protuberances, which from hereabouts have the animal aspect of warts, wens, knuckles and hips. It may indeed be likened to an enormous many limbed organism of an antediluvian time . . . Lying lifeless, and covered with a thin green cloth which hides its substance while revealing its contour.

Maiden Castle's massive quadruple ramparts are dauntingly impressive. Their outer rings encircle the hilltop for 3 kilometres (2 miles) and enclose an area of over 48 hectares (120 acres). Meticulous excavations over the last half century have shown that this was no mere military creation of one pre-Roman civilization. The chalk downland hilltop was first colonized in the Neolithic or late Stone Age and the early Bronze Age – between 3000 and 1500 BC. Though from the first it obviously afforded more than ade-

ABOVE A reconstructed gateway at the Lunt Roman fort at Baginton, Warwickshire. Maiden Castle's gates would have been of similar construction, built of wood and supporting an overhead catwalk for guards and lookouts.

OPPOSITE, ABOVE Thomas Hardy described this hilltop site as, 'An enormous many limbed organism of an antediluvian time.'

quate protection against attack, it was in fact a village set round a sanctuary dedicated to the Mother Goddess. We can see her rude effigy, along with flints, knives, axes and simple pottery, in the Dorchester Museum.

But although this is where we must go to see all remaining traces of the

earliest inhabitants of Maiden Castle, there is ample visible evidence of the vast 'Bank Barrow' which occupied the hilltop after that first village was deserted. There are reminders of this burial mound in Dorchester too, including the mutilated body of a thirty-year-old man, possibly the victim of some extraordinary ritual killing. Later there was a brief occupation of the hilltop by the Beaker

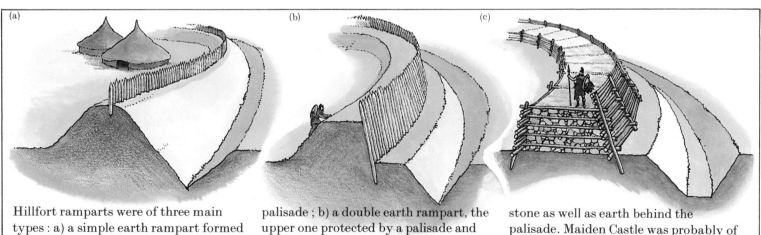

(a) (b) (c)

Hillfort ramparts were of three main types : a) a simple earth rampart formed by digging a circular ditch and piling the excavated soil around its inner edge, which was then crowned with a palisade ; b) a double earth rampart, the upper one protected by a palisade and forming a catwalk ; c) a deeper ditch and higher, vertical ramparts, given an added strength by using timber and stone as well as earth behind the palisade. Maiden Castle was probably of this last type – only more efficient, for it has quadruple ramparts instead of double.

people (so called from their drinking vessels) of whom traces have also been found, but throughout most of the Bronze Age the site was deserted, and it was not until well into the Iron Age in about 300 BC that Maiden Castle became an important fortress.

The Downs of Wessex were extensively farmed at this time, and hilltop sites afforded protection for the scattered homesteads around, and served as centres for exchange and commerce. Maiden was the most important of these, and excavations have revealed extensive evidence of third-century fortifications. They were originally strengthened by timber and protected by a ditch, but as the timber rotted it was replaced in parts by dry stone walling. There were huts, grain stores and streets within the citadel.

Over the succeeding three centuries the settlement was gradually extended, but it was at some time between 100 BC and 50 BC that Maiden Castle took on its present multi-rampart appearance. It is probable that members of the Veneti tribe from southern Brittany, refugees from the conquest by Julius Caesar, came here and inspired the creation of a major hillfort able to withstand the new siege weapon – the sling. As the effective range of the sling was around 90 metres (100 yards), defences were extended to keep the weapon out of range, and Maiden today presents a spectacle of banks and ditches around which defenders could keep constant watch. The main gateways were flanked by high limestone walls – for the defenders had their slings too, as an enormous cache of some twenty

Maiden's massive ramparts and ditches are an especially dramatic sight from the air. The gates at each end were protected by a complex system of multiple defences, which included overlapping ramparts and several outworks. An attacker seeking entrance would be forced to adopt a zigzag course which exposed him to constant fire from above.

thousand sling stones has revealed.

Maiden's defences were further strengthened, probably under the influence of Belgic settlers from Gaul, during the decades between Caesar's reconnaissance invasion and the proper coming of the Romans a century later. But these defences could not withstand the Imperial forces. The Second Legion, under the command of the future Emperor Vespasian, conquered the south and took Maiden Castle sometime during 43 or 44 AD. Archaeologists have given us a graphic picture of what happened when the east gate of the castle was stormed: many of the arrows of the artillery have been found, and in the museum at Dorchester we can see the skeleton of one of the defenders with an arrowhead in his spine. There was obviously some confusion and considerable carnage as the gates were overrun and the anger of the Roman soldiers was turned upon those who had offered stubborn resistance. Bodies of men and women showing traces of sword thrusts have been found. In the hastily prepared graves of the slaughtered, the survivors placed pots of provisions to see them through the journey after death. Here at Maiden we have what Sir Mortimer Wheeler has called 'the earliest British war cemetery'. Those who had survived the onslaught were left in relative peace, but by about 70 AD they had moved down the valley to settle around the new Roman town of Dorchester. Maiden Castle was again deserted.

It was occupied again in those 'Dark Ages' at the end of the Roman occupation of Britain, and was probably the site of a temple erected by those who refused to accept Christianity when it became the official religion of the Empire. For the last 1400 years, however, this great hilltop fortress has been uninhabited. It has merged into the contours of the landscape, its significance not fully appreciated until the coming of the archaeologists in the twentieth century.

# OLD SARUM

## WILTSHIRE

THERE IS SOMETHING PARTICULARLY evocative about vanished splendour. Lost civilizations, lost cities, even villages that have disappeared beneath the plough, have a compelling hold over the imagination. There surely can be few people who have read of Henry Bolingbroke's fateful landing at Ravenspur, at the mouth of the Humber, who do not wonder what that port, long disappeared below the waves, was like. And anyone interested in the evolution of Britain's parliamentary system will find especial fascination in those most infamous of rotten boroughs, Dunwich and Old Sarum. Dunwich is now beneath the sea and beyond recall, but on a hill over Salisbury we can still see the evidence of successive inhabitants of Old Sarum, a place which flourished until the early thirteenth century and which, deserted and depopulated, still returned two members to the House of Commons six centuries later.

Old Sarum was successively an Iron Age hillfort, Roman junction, Saxon *burgh* (or fort) and Norman castle and cathedral city, and traces of each stage of its important history are visible. Firstly, as with so many sites that have lost virtually all evidence of building above the ground, Old Sarum is best studied from aerial photographs. You then see clearly the outermost earthwork ringing the whole site. This was the Iron Age hillfort built three or four centuries before the Roman Conquest. Like Maiden, it was no mere fortress but a community gathered together on a hilltop, defended against attack and commanding views over the surrounding countryside.

Its strategic importance was obvi-

ABOVE The deep ditch and single rampart that surrounded the Iron Age settlement here around 300 years before the Roman Conquest.

RIGHT The romantic traces of a deserted city on a hilltop. At its heart is the central mound or motte, with the outline of the cathedral beyond, surrounded by the earthworks of the Iron Age fort.

ously recognized by the Romans. The site, as Sorbiodunum, was sufficiently important to be the junction of four Roman roads. In Saxon times, as Scarisbyrig, it was a major fortress against the Vikings and was used as such both by Alfred the Great (871–99) and by King Edgar (959–75). It began to rival Wilton, the old shire town, as an administrative centre and was one of the most important of the old English burghs. Part of a national system of fortifications, these were much more than mere castles on hills – rather they were stoutly defended settlements.

It was at Old Sarum, which already had a history stretching back a thousand years or more, that William the Conqueror disbanded his army in

1070, and almost immediately afterwards began work on the Norman castle. This was no orthodox motte-and-bailey castle: it was built in the centre of the Iron Age earthwork, at the heart of an old English burgh. Alongside the castle was the new cathedral built for the Bishop of Sherborne and Ramsbury.

The castle was rebuilt by the most important of those early bishops, Bishop Roger, between 1102 and 1139. He created within the Norman fortress a palatial residence very like his other palace-cum-fortress at Sherborne, in Dorset. Bishop Roger also lavished attention on the cathedral, which was extended

still further by his successor.

Roger was the most powerful man in the kingdom for many years. In the early days of Henry I's reign he controlled the administration of the entire country. An obscure priest from Avranches in Normandy, he had been noticed by the king, who was impressed by the speed with which he

ABOVE The ruins of the keep, known as the Postern Tower.

could say Mass. After his succession Henry made him Chancellor, Bishop of Salisbury and Justiciar. At a time when Church and State were almost inseparable, Roger's wealth and influence were such that his name was coupled with that of the king when royal commands were issued. He involved his family in Government: his son (the clergy did not always keep their vows) was Chancellor, his nephew, the Bishop of Ely, was Treasurer and another nephew Bishop of Lincoln. But they all fell from favour and were very harshly used by King Stephen, who took over the castle of Old Sarum and strengthened it.

Within less than a century of Roger's death, however, Old Sarum had begun its long decline into its present grassy-mounded oblivion. The cathedral was replaced by the present one, founded in 1220 at Salisbury, little over 1·5 kilometres

Bishop Roger's Palace, transformed in the early twelfth century from a Norman stronghold into a sumptuous residence fit for a man of Roger's wealth and power.

(1 mile) away, and the spaciously and classically designed medieval city, laid out on a grid plan below the hill, replaced the ancient settlement on its crowded hilltop.

Today we can trace the foundations of the old cathedral and the Bishop's Palace close by, and see something of the inner bailey of the castle, and of the stonework with which Bishop Roger replaced the timber of the first Norman castle. There are the remains too of the keep-like tower, the so-called Postern Tower, which stood apart from the main block and projected a little beyond the west curtain wall so as to command the Postern Gate on this side of the castle. There are traces of the gatehouse on the east side, and of the bake-house and a hall which was probably used by the troops from the garrison.

But all this is to the centre and west of the main enclosure which was ringed by earthworks by Iron Age warriors, developed by the Romans and re-occupied and extended by the Saxons who realized, as visitors can today, that Old Sarum was a classic hilltop site.

# TINTAGEL CASTLE

## CORNWALL

WITHOUT DOUBT there were Iron Age hillforts and cliff castles built in Cornwall. Whether there was a fortress at such an early date at Tintagel is doubtful but no book on castles would be complete without a chapter on this, the most romantic ruin in the British Isles and the one most swathed in legend. Though what survives today is mainly of Norman origin, there was certainly a monastic settlement here in the early years of the Christian era, and almost certainly some form of fortification when the fifth-century prince, upon whom the legends of Arthur were founded, ruled these parts. And the castle is no typical Norman stronghold. It has been properly called a 'Dark Age defensive position surviving into feudal times, almost in defiance of the principles of medieval architecture'.

Tintagel is set among the cliffs of the north Cornish coast. Derelict since the sixteenth century, the fortress remains an impressive sight. What gives it its special appeal is not the documented history of those who built and lived here but its long association with the story of King Arthur. It was in the middle of the twelfth century that Geoffrey of Monmouth wrote his *History of the Kings of Britain*, which first told at length the story of the British hero and linked Tintagel for ever with his name.

Geoffrey of Monmouth tells of Tintagel in the tale of Uther and Igerna. Uther Pendragon, King of the Britons, fell in love with the beautiful Igerna who was married to Gorlois, Duke of Cornwall. Gorlois objected to the attentions that the king paid his wife and returned to Cornwall with her. Uther demanded that Igerna should

It is easy to see why Geoffrey of Monmouth wrote of Tintagel, 'There is but one entrance to it and that through a rock which three men shall be able to defend against the whole power of the Kingdom'.

be returned to court, and when Gorlois refused the king invaded Cornwall. Igerna was locked away in the town of Tintagel, which Geoffrey of Monmouth describes as 'situated upon the sea and on every side surrounded by it, and there is but one entrance to it, and that through a rock which three men shall be able to defend against the whole power of the Kingdom'. Tintagel was in fact so

impregnable that it was only with the aid of the magician Merlin that Uther was able to enter the place in disguise. Merlin effected a transformation that made the king so like Gorlois that he was able to seduce the innocent

A spectacular view looking east along the coast from the island. In the foreground are the remains of St Juliot's monastery, founded in Celtic times.

24

Igerna. Gorlois was then killed in battle, Uther and Igerna married and their son Arthur was born. Geoffrey of Monmouth does not specifically say that Tintagel was King Arthur's birthplace but the association had been formed. It does not feature prominently in the Arthurian romances but it plays an important part in another medieval romance, that of Tristan, where it figures as King Mark's Castle.

In the nineteenth century the great revival of interest in the code of medieval chivalry in general, and the story of Arthur in particular, brought new fame to Tintagel. Tennyson's Arthurian poems made the legendary king's story one of the most famous and popular of the time and it was inevitable that new interest should focus on these remote clifftop ruins. It was this that led to the repair of those ruins and the creation of a new path to the site in 1852. Further interest led to further investigation, and during the last fifty years, since the ruin has been

in the care of the State, careful preservation and exploration of the site has been undertaken.

Whatever the facts behind the story of King Arthur, it is now certain that there was, at least, a Celtic monastery at Tintagel by the end of the fifth century and it was doubtless a visit to, or tales of, this remotely sited outpost of the missionary St Juliot that inspired Geoffrey of Monmouth. Traces of the monastic ruins have

been found though not of any Saxon fortress, which would certainly have been of mainly wooden construction.

The ruins we see today date from the twelfth century. This castle was begun by Reginald, an illegitimate son of Henry I. He was created Earl of Cornwall and held Tintagel until his death in 1175. He had no heir and at his death the castle passed to Prince John. When John became king in 1199 the Tintagel estates were united with the crown, and various sub-tenants held the castle until just before his death in 1216, when he granted the lands of the earldom of Cornwall to

Henry, the illegitimate son of Reginald. They reverted to the crown five years later, and in 1224 were granted to Richard, the younger brother of Henry III, who decided to take over Tintagel. He built most of the castle we see today. He was a prince of some power and influence in Europe and was elected King of the Romans, crowned with a silver crown at Aachen.

Among those who held the title Earl of Cornwall in the thirteenth century were Piers Gaveston, the notorious favourite of Edward II, and John of Eltham, brother of Edward III. Both of them neglected the castle and it was already partly in ruins before the death of Earl John. In 1337 Edward III created his eldest son, Edward (later known as the Black Prince), Duke of Cornwall, and since his day Tintagel has been among the possessions of that duchy. Towards the end of the fourteenth century, in the face of an invasion scare, the crumbling castle was refortified. It was used for a time as a prison but by the middle of the fifteenth century it was deserted again, and the long process of continuing decay had begun.

Access to the castle is still difficult for part of it is on the mainland and part is on an island. The entrance is by a path beneath a towering 82-metre (270-foot) cliff which forms the base of the upper ward. There are traces of the outer defences that protected this path and significant remains too of the main gate to the castle, above which was a chamber that was entered from the wall walk and that led to the upper ward.

The lower ward is rectangular and is enclosed on the north-east and south-east by a five-foot-thick curtain wall. The south-west is protected by the cliff. The upper ward is approached by steps cut into the rock, the top ones following the original way from the chamber above the gate. In this ward there are traces of guard rooms and two garderobes, or lavatories, opening

over the cliff face. We know from Geoffrey of Monmouth's description of the causeway, which could be defended by three men, that there was once a narrow neck of land connecting the island with the mainland. Today the only means of getting to the island is by a path on the landward side, reached by a flight of steps down the cliff face, or by one of the paths leading from the outer gate of the castle to the road.

Through a door made in 1852, when the island was opened up to visitors, one passes into the inner ward, dominated by the remains of the massive great hall. The southern end has fallen over the cliff but there are significant traces of the rest and of the series of buildings that succeeded each other on the site. At the foot of the cliff, on the north-east of the island, is a landing place guarded by a curtain wall whose gateway is still known as the Iron Gate.

On the island too are the scattered remains of St Juliot's monastery. There are traces of a primitive cell, perhaps the missionary's own, and among the monastic ruins are the remains of a Roman-style hypocaust system of underfloor heating, and of sweat houses in which the interior was heated and steam produced by pouring water on to the floors. This was thought to be a cure for rheumatic ailments.

The deep and misty past of Tintagel is all around us here. It is an historical remoteness underlined by the fact that by the time of the *Domesday Book* in 1086 there was apparently no trace of the monastery recorded. The knowledge of its presence was to be woven into the legendary history written by Geoffrey of Monmouth about half a century later.

LEFT The entrance to the island castle.

# $\mathcal{2}$ THE NORMAN

ILLIAM, DUKE OF NORMANDY, was the last invader to conquer England, and from 1066 English society began to evolve. It was not always a peaceful evolution but henceforth its upheavals were internal. William's castles were a crucial element in his success. For the castle was at once the basis of Norman military strategy and an instrument of colonization, the cornerstone of the feudal system by which William and his successors commanded and controlled their country. And it was not just England the Normans controlled. They were a remarkable people. Descended originally from Viking warriors who had settled in northern France in the tenth century, by the end of the twelfth they had established themselves from Sicily to Scotland and from Ireland to Palestine.

In the Bayeux tapestry, that most fascinating of all contemporary illustrated documents, the events leading up to the invasion, and the preparations for it, are graphically described. We see typical Norman castles in Normandy and we see that, when the invaders landed, one of the first things they did was to build themselves a castle. Wace, a chronicler from Caen, was commissioned by Henry II a century later to write a history of the invasion. He tells us that the Normans brought over a prefabricated castle with them, packed in boxes and barrels and ready for instant erection. We have no proof of this but it could well be true, for certainly they took pre-packed castles with them when they invaded Ireland a century later. The tapestry shows that one of the invaders' first actions was indeed to build a fort, set on a mound and with a ditch around it and further strengthened by a palisade. The first Norman 'castle' was at Pevensey in Sussex, and William built another at Hastings, in the same county, after the battle there. Then he built two in Kent, one at Dover and another at Canterbury.

Before taking London he crossed the Thames at Wallingford and again his men set to work on a castle. William advanced only when he had secured a base which, in real adversity, he could fall back on and which was intended to command and subdue the territory around. He did not fall back and a great wave of castle building accompanied and followed the Conquest. By the time the *Domesday Book* – the first national census and inventory – was completed in 1086, the year before William's death, a hundred castles had been built in England. The borders were heavily fortified and every major Saxon town was dominated by a Norman stronghold. The vital importance of the castle to William's strategy is best illustrated by the ruthless disregard shown towards the towns where they were built. In Lincoln 166 houses were pulled down to make way for the castle, in Norwich, Norfolk, 98 were demolished.

These hastily built castles were, like the one at Pevensey, constructed from materials that were close at hand. The earliest and very simplest consisted of little more than an artificial mound surrounded by a moat, with a palisade and sometimes a tower. These and other fortifications would be of earth and timber. As the Conquest progressed there was less urgency to build and the later castles of William's

# CASTLE

reign show a greater sophistication: the ramparts were reinforced with timber, and the walls were plastered and painted to look like stone. Indeed, before the end of William's reign, the first true stone castles were being built, and throughout the reigns of his sons, William II (William Rufus) and Henry I, the castle building continued. Many, such as Ludlow, were new stone castles and some, also like Ludlow, led to the building of a carefully planned town outside the castle gates – in Ludlow the street pattern still survives. But many of these early twelfth-century castles were replacements for the Conqueror's temporary structures. In the reign of Stephen (1135–54), a period of anarchy which the old chroniclers called the 'nineteen long winters', some of these castles played a significant part in the

A reconstruction of a typical early motte-and-bailey castle. On the motte stands a wooden keep and in the bailey are the domestic and farm buildings, a chapel and a great hall. The buildings would have been of wattle and daub construction, their roofs either thatched or timber slatted.

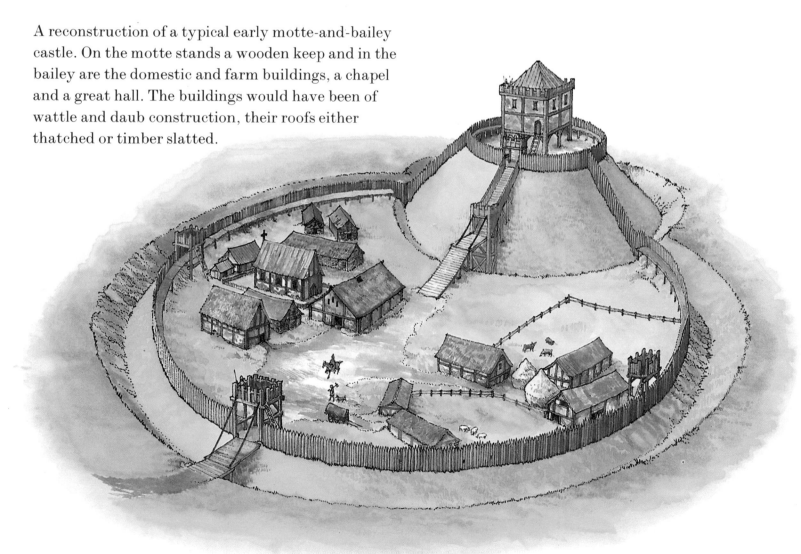

fighting which raged between the king and the Empress Matilda. For wars and rebellions were then normally determined not by battles but by siege and surrender, the reduction of an enemy's stronghold being the key to success.

Most Norman castles, whether of earth or stone, were of the type historians call motte-and-bailey castles. They consisted, like the Bayeux castles, of a fortified mound surrounded by a ditch. Beyond this first ditch would be a moat and an encircled and fortified ward, or bailey, in which would be the stables, barns, kitchens, barracks and all the other buildings needed to house a community under siege or a garrison holding down the surrounding countryside. The site would always include a good water supply. Sometimes the mound was placed in the centre of the castle, but more often it was on the circumference of the fenced bailey which housed the domestic buildings. Stone was desirable as a building material not only for its durability but because wooden buildings were naturally very vulnerable to destruction by fire or attack by battering rams.

In recent years excavations have revealed that the motte or mound itself was not always a primary feature of the castle. In some cases it appears to have been added after the construction of the central fortification or 'keep'. Doubtless, later mounds were added (as at Farnham in Surrey or Lydford in Devon) simply to strengthen the base of the keep, or to act as a deterrent against mining attack. Sometimes the bailey was enclosed by a curtain wall and its approach protected by a gate tower. Sometimes the old wooden palisade on the mound was replaced by a high stone inner wall to form what is known as a 'shell keep'. We can see examples of these keeps at Lincoln and at Berkeley in Gloucestershire.

The castle builders of the twelfth century built stone walls and towers of great height, and often the central feature of their castles was a massive rectangular keep. Such fortifications were in fact known in France in the eleventh century, but the White Tower at the Tower of London and the Great Keep at Colchester are the only English examples that date from the reign of William the Conqueror himself. Most of the square keeps in England were not built until the reign of Henry II (1154–89) when, after the anarchy of Stephen's reign, the private castles which had been built without royal permission were systematically eliminated and the country once again brought firmly under royal

ABOVE A graphic illustration of medieval warfare: the siege of Lincoln in 1217, as seen by a monastic illustrator of Matthew Paris's *Chronicle*.

ABOVE RIGHT In many parts of the country tree-clad mounds such as this are all that remain of some of the earliest Norman fortresses, especially of those built of wood. This one is at Trecastle in Powys.

ABOVE LEFT Built *c.* 1070, William fitz Osbern's hall keep at Chepstow, Gwent, was one of the earliest and finest of its type. A third storey was added in the thirteenth century, as was the upper bailey, to the left. ABOVE RIGHT The fine polygonal keep of Orford Castle, Suffolk, built by Henry II. The entrance, via the forebuilding, was raised above ground as a safety measure.

control. The right to issue licences to build castles was regarded by Henry II as very much a royal prerogative and licences were sparingly given. This in itself was an indication that after, and in spite of, the period of turbulence, the feudal pattern of society was firmly established. In the feudal system the king sat, as it were, at the top of a pyramidal society. All land was granted by him in return for service at arms, and just as all great lords owed allegiance to the king so knights owed their allegiance to the feudal lords. The castle was very much the symbol of this society, at once the home and defence of the great lord and the centre of his power, a power derived from the king. The very word used for the lord's actual dwelling in the castle indicated this. It was 'dungeon' from the French *donjon*, a word that derived from the Latin *dominium* and expressed lordship. It acquired its sinister significance only later.

The growing sophistication of military architecture throughout the twelfth century went side by side with an improvement in weaponry, especially siege weaponry. Square keeps were particularly vulnerable: their corners could be smashed or undermined and defenders had a very restricted field of fire. As a result, polygonal or cylindrical keeps were introduced; we can see examples of these at Orford in Suffolk and Conisbrough in Yorkshire. By the end of the twelfth century, however, a much more radical change was taking place, one designed to give defenders greater freedom of movement and opportunity for retaliation. The central keep was no longer the dominant feature. Much more important were the outer fortifications – stout walls with strong towers at frequent intervals. We were on the way towards those concentric defences that are the hallmark of Edward I's great castles of Wales.

# BERKELEY CASTLE
## GLOUCESTERSHIRE

IT HAS BEEN CALLED 'the most glamorous and aristocratic of English castles'. Certainly no English castle looks more beautiful than Berkeley does when seen across the meadows from the Severn, especially at sunset, when its walls take on a purple hue. No castle has had a more fascinating history either. Still lived in by the Berkeley family who built it eight hundred years ago, it has seen the brutal murder of a king and caused the longest law suit in English history. One of the earliest translators of the Bible was patronized by a Berkeley, and so was Edward Jenner, discoverer of smallpox vaccine. Shakespeare and Marlowe both wrote about Berkeley,

and the family is still forbidden by law to repair the 11-metre (35-foot) breach in its walls made by Cromwell's soldiers in the Civil War.

That breach is almost the last visible alteration to the castle, for, although within the fortress the furnishings are an elegant commentary on domestic progress through the ages, Berkeley today looks much as it has done since the fourteenth century, and is still in essence a Norman castle.

Before the Conquest the manor of Berkeley was held by Earl Godwin, father of King Harold. After 1066 the Conqueror granted Berkeley to Francis Fitz-Osborne, Earl of Hereford and Steward of Normandy,

to hold as a western outpost to defend his new kingdom. Fitz-Osborne fortified the site, but it was, as the *Domesday Book* recorded in 1086, Roger de Berkeley who first set about building a castle. Here, in 1121, Roger's son entertained Henry I. A third Roger lived here, only to be evicted after the anarchy of Stephen's reign by Henry II, who granted the castle to a distant kinsman of the de Berkeleys, Robert Fitz-Harding, who had helped him in the wars against Stephen, and who himself traced his lineage back to one of Edward the Confessor's courtiers.

There was a brief intermission in family ownership when William, Lord

ABOVE The coat of arms of the Berkeley family, who have occupied the castle, almost without interruption, for eight hundred years. It was their twelfth-century ancestor Robert Fitz-Harding who built the oldest part of the existing castle, the shell keep, in 1153. His son Maurice, second Lord Berkeley, added the forebuilding and the curtain walls of the inner and outer courtyards. The ground plan, to the right, shows these Norman buildings and also the more recent additions – the rooms that were added in the thirteenth and fourteenth centuries.

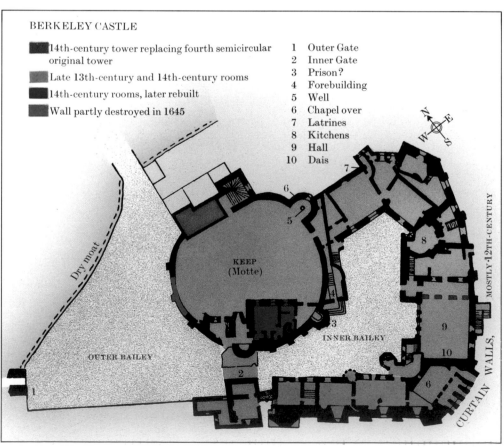

Berkeley, known as the 'waste all', gave the castle to Henry VII in

Berkeley Castle from the air, showing the close proximity of the church, and the wide breach in the wall of the shell keep which was made by Cromwell's troops. To the right of the castle are the water meadows stretching down to the Severn.

exchange for royal favours, and it remained a royal castle until the death of Edward VI, but it then reverted to the Berkeleys once more.

This was not the only strange episode in the castle's history. Because it once passed to a nephew rather than a daughter, the aggrieved female disputed the inheritance.

There was a lengthy law suit, and at one stage the family factions came to blows, fighting what is reckoned to be the last private battle on English soil, at Nibley Green in 1470.

In the eighteenth century the fifth earl became enamoured of a local butcher's daughter, Mary Cole, whose portrait is still to be seen in the castle.

Unfortunately he neglected to marry her until she was pregnant with their fifth son and then tried unsuccessfully to legitimize the other four. As a result, the fifth inherited the earldom and the first the castle. Today the owner is untitled but is a lineal descendant in the twenty-fourth generation of Robert Fitz-Harding.

The oldest part of Berkeley is the Norman shell keep, built in the middle of the twelfth century. It is 19 metres (62 feet) high and some 27 metres (90 feet) in diameter and is exceptional in two respects. Fitz-Harding chose to cut away the slopes of the existing motte and encircle it with the stone walls of his keep, so instead of a keep on top of a motte Berkeley's keep surrounds a motte. Normal entry to a shell keep was by a flight of stairs, as at Launceston in Cornwall or at York, but here the only entrance to the keep is by a small battlemented building enclosing a staircase on the inner face of the keep. Four semi-circular bastions were added but all are gone, one replaced by the fourteenth-century tower, another by a gatehouse, and two others incorporated in buildings

ABOVE The room in which Edward II was imprisoned and murdered. In a corner is a deep, well-like hole where rotting carcasses were thrown in the hope that the stench would suffocate the prisoner.
LEFT The inner courtyard. On the right is Robert Fitz-Harding's massive Norman shell keep, approached through the battlemented forebuilding, and on the left are the buildings added in the fourteenth century, with later, Tudor chimneys. The main entrance to the castle is through the gatehouse arch.
RIGHT A fourteenth-century manuscript illustration of the effete King Edward II enthroned.

inside the keep. Thomas, third Lord Berkeley, was responsible for extensive rebuilding between 1340 and 1350, creating within the inner bailey the great hall and other buildings which survive almost intact.

The most famous single event in Berkeley's history is the gruesome murder of Edward II. He was imprisoned here in May 1372, having been dethroned in a rebellion led by Earl Mortimer and his mother, Queen Isabella. In September he was done to death, attempts to poison him by throwing rotting animal carcasses into a hole by his dungeon, and other cruel indignities having failed. Tradition has it that he was murdered 'with a hoote brooch [a hot poker] putte thro the secret place posterialle', a singularly horrific death for the homosexual and ineffective king. Whether the Lord Berkeley of the time, his nominal custodian, knew of the murder is in doubt. In any event Edward III treated him with high favour and seemed to indicate that he did not hold him responsible. We can still visit the room where Edward was killed and see the deep well-like hole in the corner where the carcasses were thrown.

The castle does not have a sinister air about it, in spite of this horrible crime, and it is full of the interesting acquisitions of generations of Berkeleys. In the so-called Drake's room we can see the furniture that once belonged to Elizabeth's illustrious sailor. In the picture gallery are a number of sporting pictures to remind us that this has always been great

ABOVE The morning room, at one time the chapel, interesting mainly for its timber roof, with contemporary painted decoration. The walls are hung with a fine series of early Brussels tapestries.

hunting country. Edward I granted Thomas, Lord Berkeley, permission to hunt foxes, hares, badgers and wild cats in the surrounding land; to this day the Berkeley hunt distinguish themselves from all others by their yellow coats, renowned throughout the hunting fraternity.

Berkeley's most spectacular apartment is undoubtedly the great hall. It was built in the thirteenth century and its timbers, like those in the kitchen and above the great staircase, are worthy of special admiration. Throughout the castle there is that accumulation of furnishings, tapestries and pictures which marks the progress of a civilized and civilizing family through the centuries, and makes Berkeley not only a remarkable castle but also a great country house.

ABOVE The long drawing room, combining comfort with grandeur. The suite of gilt furniture was embroidered by the wife of the fourth Lord Berkeley; on the walls hang a fine set of mirrors.

RIGHT The magnificent great hall, built during the fourteenth century within the twelfth-century curtain wall.

38

# DOVER CASTLE

## KENT

MATTHEW PARIS, one of the most famous of all medieval chroniclers, called it 'the front door of England'. Others have called it England's 'key'. Dover Castle merits either description, guarding as it does the English cliffs at the Channel's narrowest point. It was for centuries the most vital link in the nation's maritime defences. There was an Iron Age fort here, of which the earthworks beyond the castle's outer curtain wall are almost certainly a trace. The British fleet was based here in Roman times and the Romans built a Pharos or lighthouse which still stands near the Saxon church of St Mary-in-Castro, a church that must have served the inhabitants of the Saxon burgh which was here and which contained one of the key forts of the Count of the Saxon Shore.

Within days of defeating Harold at Hastings, William the Conqueror was here and, we are told by the chroniclers, he built the first Norman castle on the site in only eight days. William regarded Dover as a site of prime importance, for it was specifically mentioned in the Oath of Allegiance which Harold gave William and which as the Bayeux tapestry shows us was the pretext for the invasion of 1066.

Odo, Bishop of Bayeux and half-brother to the Conqueror, was the first Norman constable of Dover. The castle's importance was later stressed by the fact that, unlike Old Sarum, for instance, which remained a fortified position within an ancient earthwork, Dover, having been established within the earthwork, has, over the centuries, taken it over until it completely encompasses the site both of earthwork and Saxon burgh.

Most of the great Norman castle

The core of Dover Castle is protected on three sides by a deep ditch and two curtain walls, on the fourth side by the sea. Beyond the keep can be seen the Saxon church of St Mary-in-Castro, with the Roman Pharos, or lighthouse, alongside it.

that we can see today was built after 1180 by Henry II. He spent some £7,000 – an enormous sum for the time – on commissioning Maurice the Engineer, his great castle builder, to create what was the most sophisticated castle of the day. It had many of the features of the great concentric castles of Edward I though it pre-dated them by a hundred years.

Henry's greatest achievement was

the huge square keep which still dominates the castle. It is virtually a cube in shape (30 metres by 29 metres by 29 metres – 98 feet by 96 feet by 96 feet), and its walls are between 5 metres (17 feet) and 6·5 metres (21 feet) thick. Its floors are arranged in a

OPPOSITE Henry II's great keep from the south-west, with its massive angled towers and flat buttresses.

similar way to those in the White Tower of the Tower of London, with a basement, middle floor and main floor, and a gallery above. Access to the keep is via a forebuilding as at Rochester and, again as at Rochester, the internal space in the keep is divided by a cross wall. There are four large principal rooms, each about 15 metres by 6 metres (50 feet by 20 feet), and another twelve rooms about 4·5 metres by 3 metres (15 feet by 10 feet) within the thickness of the walls.

A fine collection of armour and weaponry is displayed in one of the main rooms of the keep. Note the beautiful barrel-vaulted brick ceiling.

LEFT The huge extent of Dover's defences, seen from the north-east. On the left is the keep, surrounded by the square towers of the inner bailey wall. The capped tower in the wall enclosing the outer bailey replaced the old North Gate, breached in the siege of 1216. Henry III added the immensely strong Constable's Gate to the right. On the ridge in the foreground are 'dragon's teeth', a defence against a more recent threat – the tanks of 1940.

LEFT The huge extent of Dover's defences, seen from the north-east. On the left is the keep, surrounded by the square towers of the inner bailey wall. The capped tower in the wall enclosing the outer bailey replaced the old North Gate, breached in the siege of 1216. Henry III added the immensely strong Constable's Gate to the right. On the ridge in the foreground are 'dragon's teeth', a defence against a more recent threat – the tanks of 1940.

BELOW The Upper Chapel, one of the two beautiful Norman chapels in the forebuilding of the keep.

There are two chapels, one above the other, in the south-east angle of the forebuilding.

The keep was the core and glory of Henry's scheme, and he surrounded it by an inner curtain wall with ten wall towers, two double-towered gate-houses and two barbicans, of which all but the south barbican survive. After Henry, Richard and especially John continued to strengthen and extend the fortifications at Dover. It was John who completed the outer curtain wall round the north of the castle and built further wall towers. These were 'D' shaped rather than rectangular.

It was during John's reign that the castle saw its most dramatic action.

ABOVE Dover Castle at sunset.

The barons, who were in opposition to the king, invited Prince Louis of France to invade England and overthrow John. Louis laid siege to Dover and, in spite of its improved and massive fortifications and a spirited and formidable defence by Hubert de Burgh, he came close to taking the castle and might well have succeeded.

He did undermine the northern gateway, the eastern tower of which collapsed, but the defenders held on, and before Louis could accomplish his designs John was dead and the infant King Henry III was on the throne. At this point Louis lifted his siege and returned to France.

During Henry III's long reign (1216–72) considerable sums were spent on further extending and im-proving the castle. The outer curtain wall was extended south to the cliff head and an impressive new entrance, the Constable's Gate, was built on the west side. This replaced the under-mined northern entrance, now known as the Norfolk Towers, and is still the main entrance to the castle and the official residence of the constable.

By about 1256 the castle had reached its maximum size and most of

ABOVE Dover from the sea: a drawing of the castle, the coast and ships of the English fleet at the time of Henry VIII.

its towers were completed. An underground passage wide and high enough to accommodate a mounted knight was constructed through the chalk cliff to provide covered access to the garrison from the furthest point of the castle, and an opportunity for defenders to issue forth and take on attacking forces from behind. There were rooms to house the garrison over and around the Constable's Gate, which itself provided three tiers of firing positions for defenders at ground level, first floor level and on the ramparts above.

The castle survived in its medieval form for five hundred years, although it saw little action. Edward I was here as a prisoner of the barons before his succession, and again in 1274 when he returned from his crusades in the Holy Land. Its crucial position among the Cinque Ports – 'the gates that open and shut to the perill or safety of this Kingdome' – was recognized, and unlike many castles it was never neglected, but it saw no further action until it was taken by the Parliamentarians after a surprise attack at the beginning of the Civil War. It remained in Parliamentary hands until the Restoration and so, unlike most English castles, it was never slighted.

In the eighteenth century, however, it was significantly altered. Much of the medieval work was destroyed in the interests of making it a modern fortress. During the Napoleonic Wars, for instance, the outer wall towers were cut down and turned into gun emplacements. As late as the Second World War it was further altered so that heavy artillery could be mounted along the walls.

In spite of these architecturally unwelcome attentions over the last two centuries, Dover remains one of the most impressive medieval fortresses in Europe: much of what was erected during the reigns of Henry II, John and Henry III still remains. The keep, massive and magnificent, can still be envisaged as the royal residence that it once was.

One of the best views of the castle is from the top of the earth rampart behind the outer curtain wall on the north side. Looking back, we can see the north barbican, the inner bailey wall and the keep. But the best vantage point of all, and the most comforting for an Englishman with a sense of history, is the Channel. From there the view evokes feelings.that are enhanced by the knowledge that Dover has never been a ruin but has always served a purpose, a purpose symbolized by its list of constables who included among their number Henry V, Pitt the Younger, Wellington, Palmerston and Churchill, all fierce champions of Britain's independence.

# LUDLOW CASTLE

## SHROPSHIRE

L UDLOW is the supreme example of the border fortress. From here successive kings of England commanded the Welsh Marches. As the need for a military base was replaced by the need for an administrative headquarters, Ludlow became the seat of the Lords President of the Council of the Marches, and one of the principal centres of Government in the kingdom. But it continued to be of great strategic importance and was the last of the English castles to remain in Royalist hands in the Civil War.

Ludlow's changing role is reflected in its architectural features. Seen from the bridge over the Teme below the town, it is an impressive Norman fortress commanding the river and dominating the countryside, one of the most complete examples of medieval military architecture.

We enter the castle from the town, whose quiet, unspoilt elegance hardly prepares us for the fortifications that lie beyond the curtain wall. The castle was here before the town. In 1085 Roger de Lacy chose it as a prime site from which to subdue rough country. But de Lacy himself rebelled against William Rufus and was exiled for his pains, though not before he had built one of the first great stone keeps of the Norman Conquest.

The twelfth century was a turbulent one for Ludlow. Though the castle changed hands, it was too important to be neglected and successive occupants left their marks, the most beautiful of which is the remarkable round chapel in the middle ward of the castle, built by Sir Joyce de Dinan in the second quarter of the eleventh century. It is one of the few round

Ludlow Castle from the air, set high on a cliff and dominating the town.

churches to survive in this country and still, in spite of its ruined state, one of the finest surviving examples of medieval ecclesiastical architecture. In itself it is a reminder of the fact that the castle in those days was a community, and in it all human needs were met – physical and spiritual.

In the thirteenth and fourteenth centuries the Mortimers held Ludlow. Roger Mortimer, who had Edward II killed at Berkeley, was the first of the family to recognize Ludlow's vital strategic importance, and five generations succeeded him here until a Mortimer became king as Edward IV and made it the seat of his infant son, the Prince of Wales. This was the boy who, together with his brother the young Duke of York, met a terrible death in another fortress by the Thames, for these were the Princes in the Tower. Before their journey south, on the death of Edward IV in 1483, Ludlow had been their only home.

Ludlow, from across the Teme.

47

ABOVE It was from Ludlow that the child Princes, Edward V and his young brother the Duke of York, set out for London and the Tower in 1483, to the most tragic and perhaps most famous of royal deaths in English history. (A detail of a nineteenth-century painting by Delaroche.)

BELOW The central courtyard and the chapel from the chancel end.

Some twenty years later the castle became the home of another tragic Prince of Wales. It was to Ludlow in 1502 that Arthur, son and heir of Henry VII, brought his young bride, the Spanish Infanta, Catherine of Aragon. The marriage was a brief one. Arthur caught the plague and died in the tower that still bears his name. His young widow was too politically important a bride to be allowed either to remain in mourning or to return to Spain. Henry, the new Prince of Wales, married her – and the consequences of that marriage for English history are profound.

As we wander over the close-cropped grass where sheep now graze, we can see very clearly how this great fortress was domesticated. Within the thick Norman walls there are Tudor windows, and where we would expect to see battlements there are chimneys, all bearing witness to Ludlow's role in the sixteenth century as a great administrative centre. From here the Lords President of the Council of the Marches governed a vast territory on their sovereign's behalf. Most notable of these lords was Sir Henry Sidney, father of Philip Sidney, the poet, courtier and soldier – hero of the English Renaissance. It was Henry Sidney who was responsible for transforming the fortress into a palace. The gateway to the Judges' Lodgings still bears his arms.

The splendid and sumptuous great hall, where Sir Henry Sidney held court and which today is open to the sky, had its most glorious moment in 1634 when Milton's masque *Comus* was given its first performance to mark the Earl of Bridgwater's appointment as Lord President of the Council. Within a decade of that joyful event Ludlow was a fortress again. But there was no great Civil War siege or battle here. When the castle surrendered finally in 1646 it

was without any shots being fired. Like so many of our great castles, however, Ludlow was severely slighted by the Cromwellians in 1651. With the Restoration the Council of the Marches, which Cromwell had abolished, was restored, but it never attained its former importance and was finally disbanded in 1689 after the Revolution that brought William III to the throne.

The end of the Council marked the end of the castle's active life. Visitors who came here during the eighteenth century refer to its royal apartments, with their velvet hangings and furniture, but these were survivals of past glory. Before the end of the reign of George I in 1727 the lead had been removed from the roof, and by the

RIGHT The great hall – setting for Milton's *Comus* – and Sir Henry Sidney's lodgings, with his coat of arms over the gateway.

The entrance to the round chapel, showing the splendid Norman doorway decorated with chevron moulding.

time the castle was sold to the Earl of Powys almost a century later it was little more than a romantic ruin, much visited and often painted. Today the decay has been arrested and the castle is well maintained. Visitors wandering among the ruins can get a clearer idea here than perhaps almost anywhere else of what a major Norman fortress was like, and an idea too of how a military building could be transformed to peaceful use. Every summer Ludlow's former glory is evoked even more strongly in the central event of the annual Ludlow Festival – a Shakespearian production in the castle grounds, with the walls forming a splendid backcloth as dusk falls.

At all times and in all seasons Ludlow is a more inviting castle than most. Complete enough to satisfy the historian concerned with the development of medieval military architecture, there is nothing daunting or intimidating about it – though it still commands one of the best views over the border country which it was built to dominate and was later adapted to govern and to serve.

# ROCHESTER CASTLE

## KENT

CASTLE AND CATHEDRAL often stood close by each other in our medieval cities but nowhere is this architectural representation of the two pillars of medieval society, God and Caesar, Church and State, seen to more dramatic effect than at Rochester from across the Medway.

Rochester is one of the first. and remains one of the finest, examples of Norman military architecture. It was one of the first Conquest castles to be built entirely in stone. Its builder was Bishop Gundulf, who is best remembered for his work at the Tower of London, and much of the curtain wall which he erected upon the old Roman city wall between 1087 and 1089 – the first two years of the reign of William Rufus – still survives within the present one. Gundulf's castle consisted of an artificially levelled enclosure,

OPPOSITE The imposing twelfth-century keep, which held out for nearly two months against King John in 1215. In the foreground is the round tower built to replace the one destroyed – with the aid of the fat of forty pigs – by the king's resourceful troops.

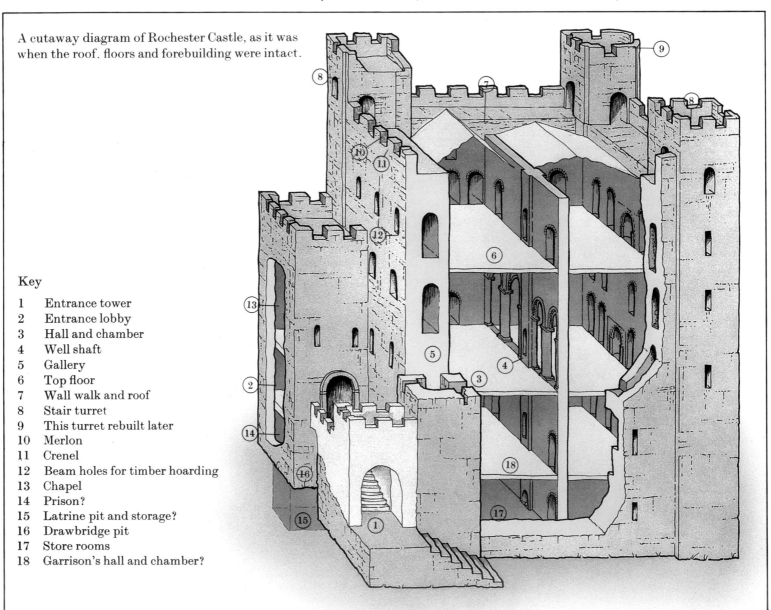

A cutaway diagram of Rochester Castle, as it was when the roof. floors and forebuilding were intact.

Key

1   Entrance tower
2   Entrance lobby
3   Hall and chamber
4   Well shaft
5   Gallery
6   Top floor
7   Wall walk and roof
8   Stair turret
9   This turret rebuilt later
10  Merlon
11  Crenel
12  Beam holes for timber hoarding
13  Chapel
14  Prison?
15  Latrine pit and storage?
16  Drawbridge pit
17  Store rooms
18  Garrison's hall and chamber?

bounded by this wall on the west or river front. It had at least one tower, a main gate-tower on the site of the present castle entrance, and a great ditch on the three landward sides.

What makes Rochester so imposing today is not the remains of that first castle but the massive keep, one of the highest and most impressive Norman keeps in England. It was built in the years following 1127, when Henry I bestowed the castle in perpetuity on William de Corbeil, Archbishop of Canterbury, and his successors, and granted him permission to 'build a fortification or tower'. The keep that William de Corbeil built survives intact, apart from its roof and floors. It is 21 metres (70 feet) square and rises 34·5 metres (113 feet) from the ground to the parapet, with corner turrets rising a further 3·6 metres (12 feet).

The walls are of Kentish ragstone with ashlar dressings and quoins from Caen in Normandy. They are 3·6 metres (12 feet) thick at the base and 3 metres (10 feet) thick at the top. The entrance at first floor level was covered and defended by a fore-building or smaller tower built on to the north face. The keep itself housed the Archbishop's apartments and a chapel. These did not interfere with its essential defensive role, nor weaken it.

It was this keep that was the subject of one of the most famous and best documented sieges in English history. In 1215 Archbishop Stephen Langton refused to surrender Rochester Castle to King John, 'in our great need'. Rebel barons seized the city to cut off the king's approach to London. This was in September of 1215, and on Monday 13 October the king himself arrived at Rochester and laid siege to the castle. For almost two months the garrison of about a hundred knights, assisted by crossbowmen and others, held out against the royal forces. Five great stone-throwing engines were brought up to bombard the walls. Though they breached the bailey they made no impact upon the keep, so the king decided to mine it. This involved

An angle of the keep. The square holes in the right-hand wall would have held beams supporting the floors of the great hall and the upper storey. Behind the arcade with a parapet is a gallery that runs within the keep's outer wall and overlooks the great hall. In the centre of the right-hand wall are the wide arches of two fireplaces.

tunnelling beneath the south-east angle and shoring up the undermined foundations with props. To fire the props John ordered his justiciar, Hubert de Burgh, to send out a writ to commandeer forty of the fattest pigs, 'of the sort least good for eating to bring fire beneath the tower'; before gunpowder came bacon fat! It did the trick and part of the keep collapsed. The cylindrical south-east turret of

the otherwise four-square tower, which was erected in conformity with the latest fashion when the keep was restored, is the pigs' permanent memorial.

The siege did not in fact end with the collapse. The defenders withdrew behind the great cross wall within the keep. 'Such was the construction of the tower', we are told, 'that the strong walls separated the half that

The interior of the keep : a view through the Norman arcade in the cross wall on the main floor. The large pier in the foreground contains the well shaft.

had fallen from the other and for several more days, until obliged by starvation to surrender, the garrison continued to resist.'

In addition to the cylindrical turret of the repaired keep, the castle was further restored, extended and improved in the sixty years that followed that siege. Among other additions, a drawbridge was provided in the southern curtain wall, a new chapel was built next to the royal apartments, stables and an almonry were erected and £50 spent on rebuilding the main outer gate.

In all well over £1,000 was spent on the castle during this period, and by 1264 it was even stronger and more imposing than it had been in 1215. It was in the Easter of 1264 that Rochester had to withstand another siege. England was once again torn by civil strife, with Henry III and his supporters on one side and some of the most prominent barons in the kingdom, led by Simon de Montfort, on the other. Rochester was held for the king,

and at Easter the Earls of Hereford and Gloucester advanced from Tonbridge and besieged the city. De Montfort advanced on Rochester from London, and at his third attempt crossed the Medway. Again bacon fat was involved in the attack, this time apparently to fire the bridge while his forces crossed over. They entered the town on Holy Saturday and after a brief truce on Easter Day directed their endeavours at William de Corbeil's great tower. It held out for a week, and then when news reached them that the king was coming to relieve the castle the besieging forces withdrew. The castle had been badly damaged, however, and during the following century of neglect it fell into decay. A hundred years later it was estimated that the repairs would cost £3,333. The only buildings left standing were the keep and some domestic offices, and they were in a state of disrepair.

Edward III, great castle builder that he was, restored and rebuilt much

of the castle, and his successor, Richard II, spent further money upon it and repaired the damage done in the Peasants' Revolt of 1381, at the beginning of his reign. After Richard's deposition the castle was again allowed to moulder and decay, and James I gave it into private hands early in the seventeenth century. In the eighteenth century there were plans for its total demolition and then a proposal to turn it into army barracks. Nothing came of either scheme, however, and just over a century ago the castle was purchased by Rochester Corporation, who spent considerable time and expense in repairing and conserving the keep and the curtain wall. In 1965 ownership was transferred to the state.

Today, in spite of the long centuries of neglect, Rochester remains one of the most interesting and impressive of Norman castles, its outstanding and dominating feature the great keep or donjon built by William de Corbeil. This massive and noble piece of architecture repays the closest study, a study which quickly disproves the notion that all was primitive and squalid within a Norman castle. Rochester, for instance, had more garderobes, or privies, than many a house built in more civilized times, and these were not its only comforts. A well was absolutely necessary in any building that was to be both residence and ultimate refuge, but in Rochester the well shaft was brought up through the cross wall within the keep, and there was a well head on each floor of the castle. Nevertheless, when the keep was determinedly besieged it was taken. It was this fall of one of the stoutest fortresses in the country that led one of the chroniclers of the time to say that afterwards, 'few cared to put their trust in castles'.

# TOWER OF LONDON

## GREATER LONDON

THERE IS no more historic fortress in Europe than this. For nine hundred years it has been London's castle, commanding the Thames and guarding the capital during times of trouble. Kings and queens have lived here and perished here. Some of the most noble and notorious characters in British history have spent their last days amid the discomfort of its forbidding dungeons.

If you want to absorb the atmosphere of the Tower – and there is no spot in the country so alive with the spirit of English history – you should go to the Ceremony of the Keys, which has been held at ten o'clock every night for more than seven hundred years, through peace and war and *blitzkrieg*. Small parties of visitors are allowed to witness this ancient ceremony when the Yeoman Warders, whose dress has scarcely altered since Tudor days, lock the Tower for the night and the cry of 'God preserve Queen Elizabeth' and the guards' 'Amen' echo through the stillness. Or go to Sunday morning service in the Chapel Royal of St Peter ad Vincula, of which Macauley said there was 'no sadder spot on earth'. Before the high altar lie, in the words of the Elizabethan John Stow, 'two Dukes between two queens, to wit, the Duke of Somerset and the Duke of Northumberland, between Queen Anne and Queen Catherine, all four beheaded'. There are over sixty men and women buried here and only nine with their heads on.

Coming from a service on a Sunday morning you are bound to see at least one of the Tower ravens outside the chapel. These enormous birds are guarded with fierce pride and devoted care by the Tower garrison, for an-

cient prophecy has it that when the ravens quit the Tower England will fall. Sunday morning too is a good time to see Tower Green, where so many of those buried in St Peter's were beheaded, including the two queens mentioned by Stow and a third, the most tragic queen of all, the seventeen-year-old Lady Jane Grey.

The Ceremony of the Keys and the regular Sunday services demonstrate that the Tower is no ruined castle or mere museum but a place where people still live and work. On such occasions you can sense the history in a way that is impossible in the long and shuffling queue which wends its way in open-mouthed admiration

ABOVE RIGHT The Ceremony of the Keys : 'Ten o'clock and all's well.'

TOP The Chapel of St Peter ad Vincula, burial place of many of the illustrious men and women beheaded on Tower Green.

OPPOSITE In winter sunlight the Tower looks especially dramatic and fortress-like. This view, from the west, shows the Norman keep, known as the White Tower, and part of the inner and outer curtain walls. On the left is the round Beauchamp Tower.

around the Crown Jewels in the Jewel House. This does not mean that you should neglect the tourist route but if you do so once you have had a chance to absorb some of the atmosphere, this unique place and its teeming history will mean much more to you. There is so much to see and ponder at that in a lifetime of regular visits you will see and learn something new each time.

The Tower was founded by William the Conqueror. Here, in 1066, he built an earthwork at the south-east corner of the eastern wall enclosing the City of London, from which he could command the capital of his newly conquered kingdom. But the earthwork was merely a temporary expedient. Before his reign was out a massive fortress was well under construction. He made Gundulf, a monk from Bec in Normandy, his Clerk of Works. Gundulf later became Bishop of Rochester and was responsible for the construction of that mighty castle too.

Work continued during the reign of William Rufus and Henry I and during the anarchy of the civil wars between Stephen and Matilda – 'these nineteen long winters' – when the Earl of Essex, who was Constable of the Tower, ruled London. When he fell into Stephen's hands the Tower was his ransom and the means whereby the citizens of London regained their liberty. At the end of the twelfth century, in 1191, the Tower was surrendered by Richard I's regent, while he was absent on the Crusades, to the citizens led by Prince John. When John was on the throne the Tower was held in pledge pending the sealing of Magna Carta. 'The Tower' was the White Tower, one of the finest and largest keeps in western Europe, and still today, in spite of medieval embellishments and windows added by Christopher Wren, essentially a Norman building. This was Gundulf's tower, built of white stone from Caen, but owing its name to the greater whiteness bestowed on it by Henry III who whitewashed it all over, within and without.

Successive kings added to the fortifications. In spite of his long absence – and he spent less than a year of his ten year reign in his kingdom – Richard I lavished money on it. Henry III made it his principal residence and built most of the great circle of flanking towers that form the inner curtain, transforming it, in effect, into one of the earliest concentric castles.

In addition to his fortifying and whitewashing endeavours, Henry also rebuilt the royal apartments and a house for an elephant with which he was presented. This was the beginning of the Royal Menagerie House, in and around the Lion Tower (where the bookshop and refreshment room are now), which was here from the thir-

teenth century until 1834. Kings and princes took great pride in the exotic animals captured for them or presented to them.

Henry III's son, Edward I, the greatest of all our castle building monarchs, did not neglect the Tower. He built the outer curtain wall and towers, and much of his work survives. Indeed we approach the Tower by his entrance from the City, through the Middle Tower and across the bridge over the moat, now dry but once full of water – so foul that citizens bathed there on pain of death. We pass through the Byward Tower, the gatehouse of the outer ward, and by the Bell Tower where Bishop Fisher of Rochester, Sir Thomas More and the Duke of Monmouth spent their last days, and where the young Princess Elizabeth was imprisoned for a time. In the curtain wall, east of the Bell Tower, are the windows of the Lieutenant's Lodgings, now called the Queen's House. One of them is the window of the Council Chamber where Guy Fawkes, of the Gunpowder Plot, was examined before his trial at Westminster.

On the river side at this point is the most famous of all the entrances to the Tower, Traitor's Gate, beneath St Thomas's Tower. It is a strange irony that beneath the tower named after the most revered of English martyrs, and containing an oratory dedicated to him, successive state prisoners came through the river gate from their trials at Westminster. Not all prisoners failed to re-emerge. The very first man ever imprisoned in the Tower, Ranulf Flambard, Bishop of Durham, escaped in 1101 because he managed to have a rope smuggled to him in a jar of wine and simply let himself out of the White Tower. During the wars with France, David, King of the Scots, John, King of France, Charles of Blois and other illustrious prisoners were lodged there. Perhaps the most famous of all escapes from the Tower was that of Lord Nithsdale, one of the Jacobite lords captured after the 1715 rebellion. Dressed as his wife's maid, he was spirited out of the Devereux Tower on the eve of his execution.

Opposite Traitor's Gate is the Bloody Tower, so known since the late sixteenth century, probably because Henry Percy, eighth Earl of Northumberland, committed suicide here. This is also the tower in which, by tradition, the two infant princes, Edward v and his brother the Duke of York, were murdered in 1483. It was here too that Sir Walter Raleigh was imprisoned for twelve years. Just beyond is the Wakefield Tower, named after William Wakefield, clerk to Edward III. Here, in the small chapel, Henry VI, last Lancastrian king and patron of the arts, was murdered. Every year tributes of roses and lilies from his two great foundations, Eton and King's, Cambridge, are laid in his honour on 21 May.

All of these towers date from the thirteenth century. By then the Tower of London was the strongest fortress in England and covered virtually all of its present 7-hectare (18-acre) site. Its historical associations are not all

The tranquil and beautiful chapel of St John the Evangelist, in the south-east corner of the Tower. Its domed, apsidal shape is repeated in the tiers of high Norman arches.

sinister or sombre. Until the reign of Henry VIII kings maintained residences here, and every monarch before James I stayed here before the coronation and went forth in triumphal progress to Westminster. For centuries the Royal Mint was housed at the Tower, the nation's coinage protected in imposing style. It housed the Public Record Office too and, briefly, the Royal Observatory. The Crown Jewels have been safely kept here for centuries, though in the reign of Charles II a Colonel Blood made an attempt to steal them, an extraordinary episode that was made even more extraordinary by the fact that the king he had sought to plunder behaved with remarkable indulgence, restoring to him his confiscated estate in Ireland and bestowing other marks of favour. Perhaps there was a special meaning in Blood's words, 'it was a bold attempt but it was for a Crown'.

in 1540 by the king who divorced her. In the Salt Tower – perhaps the most interesting of all – is the astronomical clock carved by Hew Draper, imprisoned for witchcraft in 1561.

These are not the only writings associated with the Tower. It was here that Thomas More wrote two of his most famous essays, and Walter Raleigh, during his long imprisonment, his *History of the World*. It was a book about the Tower, *The Tower of London* by Harrison Ainsworth, published in 1840, that aroused a new and public curiosity in this most ancient and historic of English castles. It was a curiosity that was satisfied in 1875 when, for the first time, the whole Tower was opened to the public. Today it is the most visited monument in Britain. Its armouries, the

The room in the Bloody Tower in which Sir Walter Raleigh was imprisoned. It was here that he wrote his *History of the World*.

The moving inscription carved by John Dudley, Earl of Warwick, during his years of imprisonment in the Beauchamp Tower.

oldest museum in the country, where some of the exhibits have been on show for more than four hundred years, are visited by millions. In 1978 a splendid new history gallery was opened to mark the Tower's 900th anniversary. It traces the story of this most fascinating of buildings from the time of William the Conqueror to the nineteenth-century restorations by Salvin and beyond.

Charles II never lived in the Tower for Cromwell demolished the royal apartments, including the great hall where Anne Boleyn had been tried. It remained a state prison, however, throughout the eighteenth century and has been used as such since. Roger Casement was housed here during the First World War and Rudolf Hess (briefly) in the Second. In the Beauchamp Tower and the Salt Tower, once known as Julius Caesar's

Tower, there are some very poignant prisoners' inscriptions. Over the fireplace in the Beauchamp is the signature, 'Arundel, June 22nd, 1587'. Philip Howard, son of the Duke of Norfolk, himself beheaded in 1572, scratched in Latin, 'The more suffering for Christ in this world, the more Glory with Christ in the next'. In the Beauchamp too is the monogram of Thomas Abell, servant and chaplain to Catherine of Aragon and beheaded

# 3 THE CLIMAX OF CASTLE

AMONG THE MANY ROYAL tombs in Westminster Abbey is a plain black one without an effigy which marks the final resting place of one of the most powerful and significant of our kings. It bears the simple inscription, '*Edwardus Primus : Scotorum Malleus : Pactum Serva*' – 'Edward I : Hammer of the Scots : Keep Troth'. It is a pity that there is no effigy for we know he was a noble figure of a man, tall and handsome with a broad brow and a fair face and a mass of hair which turned snow white with age. He was thirty-three when he came to the throne, and during his long reign (1272–1307) he did more than any other king since the Conqueror to set his stamp upon his country. He transformed Britain's legal system, and he began the regular practice of summoning both Lords and Commons to his Parliament. He was a man of devotion and fidelity whose love for his wife caused him at her death to set up a cross at each place where her body lay on its journey from Hadby in Lincolnshire to Charing Cross. He was a tough man too, skilled in the chase and the tournament and well blooded on the battlefield. He campaigned against the French, Scots and Welsh, and when he died he left a near bankrupt Exchequer and a series of the greatest castles ever built.

Most of our medieval monarchs, with the significant exception of Edward II and Richard II, both of whom were murdered in castle prisons, were great castle builders, but Edward I was without doubt the greatest of them all, and his mighty Welsh fortresses are still among the most renowned and most visited of all the castles in Britain. He built ten castles in Wales during his campaigns to subdue the Welsh, and most stand to this day as awesome reminders of his power and resolution.

Edward's castles were not just great castles : they were a new development in military architecture in Britain. Before coming to the throne Edward had gone on crusade to the Holy Land. He had seen the great walls of Constantinople and other fortresses of the Byzantine Empire. He had seen great crusader castles such as Krak des Chevaliers in Syria and had himself relieved Acre and won a victory at Haifa. On his way home he stayed with his uncle, Philip I of Savoy, and there met Philip's architect, Master James of St George. He was the man who became Edward's master builder and had a hand in almost every major castle built by Edward during his reign.

The castles of the Byzantine Empire and the eastern crusader castles that were modelled on them were markedly different from the Norman motte-and-bailey castles. They were concentric castles, the central buildings of the castle protected by two well spaced curtain walls, the outer overlooked and protected by the inner. It was not a new idea – it had been used by the Egyptians two thousand years before the birth of Christ and the pattern was followed in those fourth-century walls at Constantinople which Edward must have marvelled at.

Caerphilly, in Glamorgan, was built by a powerful nobleman. It was Britain's first concentric castle, and the largest castle in Wales. At its heart is an inner enclosure with huge round corner towers and two

# BUILDING

RIGHT Edward I, Hammer of the Scots, greatest of all castle building English kings, seen in peaceful, contemplative mood, surrounded by monks and bishops.

twin-towered gatehouses, surrounded by a second walled enclosure set in an artificial lake. The other great concentric castles, however, were Edward's. Most spectacular of all is Caernarvon, in Gwynedd, the castle he began in 1283 beside the Menai Strait. Edward saw it not only as a military stronghold but also as a symbol of his conquest of Wales, and it was here, according to tradition, that he presented his son to the Welsh people as their new prince in 1301. At Conway in Gwynedd Edward built the town wall at the same time as his castle. With its twenty-one towers and three double-towered gateways it is by far the most outstanding example of a medieval town wall remaining in Britain. The castle itself was mainly completed in the four years between 1283 and 1287. It has eight huge towers and has been called the most compact assembly of turretry in the British Isles. The towers are over 9 metres (30 feet) in diameter with walls up to 4·5 metres (15 feet) thick. Each one is over 21 metres (70 feet) high with several storeys containing rooms and a staircase. One of them is known as the prison tower and has a concealed dungeon where the only light or air would come by way of a 46-centimetre (18-inch) square shaft passing through a 3·6-metre (12-foot) wall.

Seven years after Conway was completed, in 1294, Prince Madog Ap Llewelyn led a rebellion against English rule in Wales. His troops attacked Edward's castles and caused much damage, especially at Caernarvon. Edward marched to North Wales and established his base at Conway. Almost as soon as he arrived, the river rose and he was trapped in the castle, his supply line severed. There he and his men had to eke out a bare existence on a diet of salted meat, coarse bread and foul water until the river subsided. When it did, Edward emerged to crush the rebellion and to order the building of another

ABOVE LEFT The great concentric castle of Beaumaris on the Isle of Anglesey.

ABOVE RIGHT Harlech Castle, Gwynedd, looking across the inner courtyard and showing the inner face of the keep-gatehouse. It was the last bastion of Owen Glendower in the struggle between the Welsh and Henry IV.

castle on the Isle of Anglesey itself, across the Menai Strait, further strengthening his hold over Wales.

This other castle was Beaumaris in Gwynedd and it is the most perfect of all the castles of Master James, a piece of military precision engineering incorporating the very latest ideas. It has a square inner bailey flanked by eight rounded towers, four of which also served as a gatehouse protecting the two entrances on opposite sides of the bailey. Gone is the keep. Each of the gatehouses is massive enough to contain comfortable rooms for the lord of the castle, but each on its own is capable of fulfilling the function of the keep, that of a separate defensible unit. Even if attackers could fight their way through the archway under the gatehouse, they would only emerge on the other side of the bailey with the gatehouse itself intact behind and above them. At that point the extra flanking towers on the inner side of the gatehouse would come into their own, protecting it against its own courtyard. Any enemy who succeeded in overwhelming the first line of defence would be in possession only of a narrow strip of land in which he was extremely vulnerable from yet higher walls ahead. The measure of its success as a deterrent fortress is that no one ever needed to fire a shot in its defence.

Edward's Welsh castles are the summit of medieval military architecture. One of the principal reasons for this is that elsewhere there was rarely the chance to build a great castle from new; it was more frequently a case of adding to or strengthening what had been inherited, although a number of English castles, including the Tower of London, were made concentric during Edward's reign. Master James himself was one of the most notable of all medieval architects. He was given a position of great prominence by the king and styled as 'Master of the King's Works in Wales'. His pay was 3s a day, which was an enormous figure for those times, and in addition he was leased royal manors at a low rent and given other 'perks'. Edward recruited a remarkable body of craftsmen, including Stephen the Painter who had worked on the redecoration of Westminster Hall, and Thomas Houghton who had

RIGHT The art of siege: a Muslim town is attacked by Crusaders using stone-throwing catapults to break down the walls. The garrison defends itself by shooting arrows and hurling missiles, but a tower crumbles under the assault.

built the canopy for the tomb of Edward's wife Eleanor in Westminster Abbey. These and other craftsmen, some of whom were paid as much as 3s 6d a week, were the leaders of an army of some three thousand workmen recruited from England. When Aberystwyth in Dyfed and Rhuddlan in Clwyd were built Edward sent writs all over England instructing sheriffs to dispatch workmen to Wales. And Harlech in Gwynedd – another of his great concentric castles – was built with English labour: the original Men of Harlech were not local men.

It was necessary that castles should be strong and stout, for methods and weapons of attack had developed significantly. We can learn a great deal about techniques of medieval warfare from the writings of the old historians or chroniclers, and from illuminations in early manuscripts. The main methods of attack were either a direct assault over the curtain wall, bombardment to cause a breach in defences, mining, or blockade to starve the defenders into submission. In the direct assault attackers used ladders and battering rams, and for bombardment the ballista, a giant crossbow mounted on a stand, which discharged iron darts. There was also the mangonel, a huge catapult designed to hurl stones and other heavy missiles at gates and walls, and the trebuchet, a somewhat similar missile hurler which used a giant sling and could hurl a stone weighing 150 kg (320 pounds) at least 100 metres (330 feet). Sometimes these machines discharged 'Greek Fire', which has been called a medieval version of the napalm bomb. Although it could not penetrate stonework it was deadly against men and horses and combustible materials. One of the most effective weapons of all was the tunnel or mine, such as the one that brought down the keep at Rochester in 1215. A variation was for the attacker to try to obtain access through a latrine drain or chute or some other such opening. Richard I's great Chateau Gaillard, the most famous of all the Normandy castles, was taken this way in 1204. All of these methods were much more difficult to operate against the concentric castle, well manned by men with bows and crossbows. Incidentally, though hot liquids were sometimes discharged on to the heads of attackers who got too close, boiling oil was a bizarre figment of the imagination.

The most effective way of taking a castle, and the least costly in terms of the attackers' lives and effort, was to seek to starve it into submission, and that was the method that attackers increasingly used when faced with apparently impenetrable defences such as Edward had just created in Wales.

Although all fighting had by no means come to an end by the fourteenth century – and though England was yet to suffer two Civil Wars, one of them very prolonged – there was, as the century unfolded, an increasing desire on the part of those who built castles to concentrate on the comfort and convenience of their inhabitants, and in so doing to recognize that the conditions of the time allowed an Englishman's castle to become his home.

# CAERNARVON CASTLE
## GWYNEDD

D R JOHNSON called it 'an edifice of stupendous majesty and strength', and the Welsh historian Thomas Pennant, 'the most magnificent badge of our subjection'. There is certainly no more imposing castle in the British Isles than Caernarvon. It is the noblest of that great quartet of Edwardian castles – Harlech, Conway and Beaumaris are the others – built by Edward I to mark his domination of Wales.

The site was chosen not only for its strategic importance but for its symbolism. Here, by the Menai Strait, Edward wanted to signal his conquest of Wales, for it was not only a

commanding site, it was one that enabled him to administer his dominions from the place where the Romans had established the north-west outpost of their empire. For this was the site of Segontium, an appropriate place for a new imperial ruler to mark his claims and hold his conquest. In 1283, the year when Edward began to build, a body was unearthed at Caernarvon which was believed to be that of the Emperor Magnus Maximus, allegedly Constantine I's great nephew. Stories were told in Wales of his having dreamt of coming from Rome to a land of mountains where a river flowed into the sea, and

Caernarvon, one of the most impressive and most symbolic of all British castles, built by Edward I to re-establish a Norman conquest and to fulfil a legend. Among its characteristic features are its cross-banded masonry and strong polygonal towers.

finding 'a great fort, the fairest that man ever saw, and great towers of many colours, and in its hall a chair of ivory surmounted by two eagles of gold'.

The castle that Edward built was meant to fulfil the tradition and interpret the dream. This explains why Caernarvon looks so different from any other castle in Wales, with

The Investiture of the Prince of Wales in 1969. The first heir to the throne to bear that title was the son of Edward I and Queen Eleanor, born at Caernarvon in 1284.

its polygonal towers and cross-banded masonry, based on the Theodosian wall at Constantinople, Constantine's own city. Symbolism did not end here. Edward deliberately incorporated within his castle the motte of a former Norman castle, thus seeking to establish that in holding Wales he was asserting an ancient right and not merely celebrating a new conquest.

Though Caernarvon was not finished at Edward's death in 1307, and indeed was never fully completed, it is the largest and most impressive of his castles. He intended it as a royal residence as well as an imperial fortress and contrived to have his queen, Eleanor, bear their first-born child there in April 1284. This was the boy he proclaimed as the first English Prince of Wales, a title that has been borne by most heirs to the throne ever since. It was here at Caernarvon that a new custom was created in 1911 when another Edward, Prince of Wales, was invested during a colourful medieval-style ceremony and presented to the people as their prince by his father George V. That ceremony was created by Lloyd George, who had had himself made Constable of Caernarvon, a borough he represented in Parliament for over fifty years. In 1969 a similar investiture was held for the present Prince of Wales.

Caernarvon is not a true concentric castle because of its site. Its walls form a narrow, waisted enclosure shaped like an hour-glass, a shape determined partly by the rock on which it was built, and partly by the moat of the earlier Norman castle which Edward deliberately retained in the upper bailey. The castle is united into an integrated whole by a magnificent series of thirteen polygonal towers, so sited as to provide cover for the whole circumference. It was a formidable fortress with two firing galleries along

the whole of the south front, one above the other, fixed in the thickness of the wall. These, combined with the crenellated walls and towers, provided an unsurpassed fire power.

The most commanding of the towers is the Eagle Tower, which originally bore a stone eagle on each of its three turrets (another symbolic reminder of might in this use of the

emblem of the Roman army). This tower, at 36·5 metres (120 feet), was the highest of medieval castle towers. Within it were the apartments of the king's Viceroy, Otto de Grandison, who at the end of the thirteenth century was paid the fabulous sum of £1,000 for controlling Wales, and another £100 for holding Caernarvon. There is little doubt that Edward

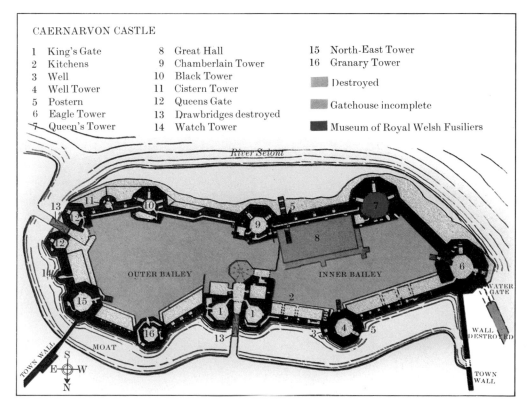

CAERNARVON CASTLE

1  King's Gate
2  Kitchens
3  Well
4  Well Tower
5  Postern
6  Eagle Tower
7  Queen's Tower

8  Great Hall
9  Chamberlain Tower
10  Black Tower
11  Cistern Tower
12  Queens Gate
13  Drawbridges destroyed
14  Watch Tower

15  North-East Tower
16  Granary Tower

Destroyed

Gatehouse incomplete

Museum of Royal Welsh Fusiliers

intended these apartments as the future home of the Prince of Wales too, and throughout the castle there were sumptuous rooms suitable for the king to use on his progress through this part of his dominions.

The royal apartments in the inner or upper bailey were never completed, nor were the buildings that were designed to separate them from the outer or lower bailey. In addition to the watergate in the Eagle Tower, there were two main gateways to the castle, each with two towers flanking the entrance passage. The Queen's Gate at the east end, never completed, leads into the royal inner bailey, which is approached across a drawbridge. The King's Gate on the north front is the main entrance from the fortified town. Caernarvon was walled at the same time as the castle was built, the two making an integrated defensive unit, as at Conway. No building in Britain, it has been said, 'exhibits more strikingly the immense strength of medieval fortifications' than the King's Gate. A drawbridge crossed the northern moat, and five massive doors and six portcullises then barred the way. There was to have been a further drawbridge beyond. Anyone approaching could be covered all the way from firing loops and spy holes at different levels. There are no less than nine surviving 'murder holes' above the portcullises from which objects could be unleashed on attackers.

Edward began Caernarvon in 1283, pressing men into service and spending the equivalent in today's currency of many millions over the years. In 1294 he suffered a serious reverse when the Welsh revolted under Madog, one of their native champions, but the castle was quickly retaken and building continued. It was probably as a result of this setback that Master

The castle and part of the walled town of Caernarvon. The Eagle Tower, on the far right, stands proud, a fortress in itself. In the distance are the Menai Straits and the hills of Snowdonia.

ABOVE A wall-walk, the outer face (right) pierced with defensive embrasures.

LEFT The view from the Eagle Tower, in the upper bailey, to the Queen's Gate, at the end of the lower bailey. On the right are the foundations of the great hall, with the Chamberlain Tower beyond; on the left is the King's Gate.

James of St George, the great military engineer and architect from Savoy who was in charge of Caernarvon, designed the elaborate fortifications of the King's Gate.

Shortly afterwards Edward, distracted by his Scottish adventures, turned his attention away from Caernarvon, and when he died in 1307 the castle was far from complete. Work continued between 1309 and 1330, but it still remained unfinished.

Little can have been done to increase the comforts of the castle in the next fifty years for when Richard II came here in 1399 we are told he had to sleep on straw. However, the effectiveness of its defences was proved when Owen Glendower lost three hundred men trying to take the castle in 1401. He failed again in 1402 and 1403 in spite of the fact that he used massive siege equipment on the last occasion and the garrison consisted of only twenty-eight men.

Caernarvon next featured prominently in history in the seventeenth century. Puritan prisoners, including Prynne, the pamphleteer, were imprisoned here. During the Civil War the castle changed hands three times but without major action. Though there were orders for its demolition after the Restoration they were, happily, never carried out, and in the nineteenth century it was restored, at public expense, by Salvin.

Today the castle looks remarkably undamaged from the outside although it is in fact a shell. It is well worth a long and careful visit, however, for in spite of the ruined state of its interior Caernarvon still has the massive grandeur that so impressed men through the ages, and still conveys a clear idea of Edward's grand design. It is perhaps best seen from the ramparts of the great southern curtain wall and from the top of the Eagle Tower, which provides a panoramic view of the whole castle.

# CAERPHILLY CASTLE

## MID-GLAMORGAN

THANKS TO CAREFUL and sensitive restoration by two rich noblemen at the end of the last century·and the beginning of this, we can appreciate to the full the greatest castle erected by any nobleman of the Middle Ages. Caerphilly is positively awe-inspiring. The largest of all British castles after Windsor, its fortifications cover 12 hectares (30 acres). It was privately built, and the building operations are poorly documented, but Caerphilly exceeds the great Welsh castles of Edward I in size and strength and rivalled them in the splendour of its architecture and the luxury of its apartments. Unlike Edward's two greatest castles, Beaumaris and Caernarvon, it was completed, and completed within a remarkably short space of time. It was begun soon after 1270 and was almost certainly finished within the decade; only the great hall was remodelled later – sometime around 1326. It not only rivalled the great Edwardian castles, therefore, it pre-dated them.

Its builder was Gilbert de Clare, head of the most powerful family in the kingdom. Lord of Glamorgan, Earl of Gloucester and of Hereford, he built Caerphilly to establish his hold over his Welsh territory and to contain his great rival Llewelyn ap

It is easy to see why Caerphilly, with its elaborate fortifications set in a vast expanse of water. was one of the most formidable strongholds in Europe.

Gruffyd, the last of the great Welsh Princes. There had been a fortress on this site in Roman times, and during the eleventh century a simple motte-and-bailey castle. Gilbert's first attempt at fortifying the site was destroyed by Llewellyn in 1268. By 1270 he was building a major castle to contain his enemy's aggression and end the battering of the greatest siege engines Llewellyn could produce.

Gilbert erected a castle that has been ranked among the finest military architecture in Europe. Caerphilly is quite simply one of the greatest buildings of the Middle Ages, equal in importance to any of Britain's major cathedrals. There never was a more triumphant assertion of power and magnificence by any noble subject. The state apartments were of royal splendour. The need for military

The fortress from the south lake, showing the watergate in the outer curtain wall and the flanking towers of the inner ward.

The inner ward, looking west towards the inner gatehouse. The cylindrical north-west tower stands on the right and the great hall on the left. In the central foreground is the well.

strength did not exclude a substantial measure of domestic comfort, though of that comfort there is no trace today.

The military might of Caerphilly is so obvious that one tends to forget that its site was not a commanding one. There were no natural advantages to be exploited here, so Gilbert made his castle doubly secure, first by a series of concentric fortifications, secondly by a great expanse of water. In this he was doubtless inspired by the way in which artificial lakes had prolonged Henry III's siege at Kenilworth during the wars against de Montfort's barons a few years previously. Though the design, and particularly the use, of flanking towers and gate towers was foreshadowed a hundred years before at Dover and at

Richard's great castle, Chateau Gaillard in Normandy, Caerphilly was the first truly concentric castle on British soil.

Its outer ward forms a surrounding platform held in by a low, crenellated outer curtain. There are two gatehouses, each with twin towers, and a watergate in the south front, next to the kitchen tower in the inner bailey. The main stronghold of the castle is the inner ward, a regular rectangular enclosure bound together by two gatehouses to east and west, the kitchen tower, and four mighty cylindrical towers at the four angles, each of which could be held separately.

On the south side of the inner court are the hall and other apartments, and there was further accommodation in the towers and gatehouses. The unique feature of Caerphilly is its eastern front, a long screen of curtain walls and platforms strengthened by turrets and buttresses. By a magnificent feat of engineering, the valley in which the castle stood was turned into a great artificial lake held in by a fortified dam 364 metres (400 yards) long, which served not only to hold in the water but to give extra defences to the castle. This dam was crossed from the outer entrance which bars the main approach to the castle. Originally there was a further line of defence consisting of an island to the west, with a drawbridge entrance guarded by two projecting bastions and connected with the main castle by a

Just the first of Caerphilly's many lines of defence – the long, buttressed screen on the east front, which also serves as a dam to contain the waters of the lake.

further drawbridge to the outer western gate.

But by the time Caerphilly was completed it was in effect obsolete, for by the end of the thirteenth century Wales had been effectively subdued, and a fortress on this scale was no longer necessary to cope with the minor revolts and skirmishes that punctuated Anglo-Welsh relations over the next century or so.

Its history was uneventful but not entirely without incident. Edward II took refuge at Caerphilly during his

The outer drawbridge and gatehouse on the east side of the castle, with the northern end of the fortified dam in the foreground.

unsuccessful struggle against his mother, Isabella, when his favourite, Hugh Despenser, held it. Edward was defeated and later murdered at Berkeley, and Despenser was beheaded. Thereafter the castle saw little further excitement, although it served as an administrative centre and Owen Glendower held it briefly during his rebellion against Henry IV at the beginning of the fifteenth century. By the middle of the sixteenth century the northern tower was being used as a prison, but most of the rest of the castle was in ruin, even serving as a quarry from which a local worthy, Thomas Lewis, built his house.

In the Civil War its defences were deliberately damaged still further to make it of little attraction to the Royalist forces, its owner being a

Caerphilly from the east. In the foreground is the fortified dam and the bridge to the outer ward. Enclosing the inner ward are the corner towers and the twin-towered eastern gatehouse. The dramatically precarious angle of the south-east tower was almost certainly the result of mining in the Civil War.

Parliamentarian. The famous leaning south-east tower is almost certainly a memorial of Civil War gunpowder, although there is a more colourful legend which has it that the tower was damaged in an explosion at the time of Isabella's attack.

The castle was in a sorry and overgrown state when the third Marquess of Bute, better known for his rebuilding at Cardiff and Castell Coch, began restoring it soon after his succession in 1868. His son, the fourth marquess, continued the work at the beginning of this century, concentrating on trying to make the castle look as much like the thirteenth-century original as possible. The Butes were particularly successful in restoring the water defences. There was no question of allowing guesswork or conjecture to take over, and the castle that was handed over to the state by the fifth marquess in 1950 was, to all outside appearances, much as it must have looked on its completion 700 years before.

Caerphilly is a castle to which one must devote considerable time, guide book in hand, for there is no finer or more fascinating example of military architecture in the country.

# GOODRICH CASTLE

### HEREFORD AND WORCESTER

GOODRICH seems to grow from the living rock on which it stands. If Caerphilly shows how medieval builders made massive defences without natural advantage, Goodrich is perhaps the supreme example of taking advantage of a natural strategic position.

Perched on a high crag, this red sandstone border fortress guards one of the most important crossings of the Wye between England and Wales. Goodric's Castle – named after a local lord – lies in territory conquered from the Welsh soon after the Norman invasion. There are records of a castle here as early as 1101 but nothing of that first fortress now remains.

The earliest part of the present castle is the small compact keep, only some 9 metres (30 feet) square, which was built around the middle of the twelfth century. It is a fine and simple example of a Norman keep arranged in three storeys, with the original entrance (later converted to a window) on the first floor. At the beginning of the thirteenth century a curtain wall with angled towers was added. Somewhere around 1280 all but the keep was swept away and a new castle built. The builder was the king's uncle, William de Valence, a half-brother of Henry III and a man of some importance. He created a rectangular castle about 46 metres by 38 metres (150 feet by 125 feet) in size. On three corners were projecting towers and the fourth, the north-east, was occupied by the gatehouse, on one side of which was a D-shaped chapel tower, and on the other a small circular turret. This remains much as he built

RIGHT Goodrich, on its strategic clifftop site above the River Wye.

it, although the chapel window is a fifteenth-century addition. The entrance passage, which originally had a

BELOW RIGHT *The natural chasm that is Goodrich's greatest defence. Rising from the floor of the moat is the south-east corner tower with its huge, angled buttresses.*

portcullis at each end, leads into the courtyard which contains the various castle buildings. To the west are the remains of the great hall, with its adjoining kitchen. Linked to the great hall were the basement and ground floor of the south-west tower, used for storage of food and drink.

Beside the great hall were the

owner's apartments, including a fine solar and a private chapel, the other chapel being for the general use of the garrison, who also probably occupied the other buildings to the east of the courtyard.

The rock on which the castle stands is cleft by a natural chasm which was transformed into a wide and deep-cut

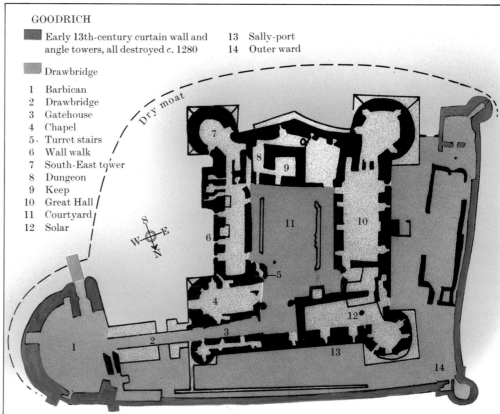

GOODRICH

■ Early 13th-century curtain wall and angle towers, all destroyed *c.* 1280

Drawbridge

1  Barbican
2  Drawbridge
3  Gatehouse
4  Chapel
5  Turret stairs
6  Wall walk
7  South-East tower
8  Dungeon
9  Keep
10  Great Hall
11  Courtyard
12  Solar
13  Sally-port
14  Outer ward

Next to the great hall were William de Valence's private apartments, including a fine solar in the upper storey. Though its floor no longer exists, the slender pier that rises through two storeys to support twin Gothic arches is still intact. In the left foreground is the well.

moat. Opposite the gatehouse is the massive barbican, itself originally surrounded by a curtain wall. Barbicans were designed to keep the enemy at a distance, forming an outer defence which had to be taken before the main castle could be attacked. Goodrich's barbican was based on one created by Edward I at the Tower of London between 1275 and 1276. It is of a similar half-moon shape and was built later than the rest of the castle, probably during the decade from 1310 to 1320. As with the Tower, it could only be reached by a narrow bridge across the moat, and any attacker would be forced to turn at right angles and be subjected all the time to fire from the main castle, which could only be reached over a further bridge.

Because of its crag site, Goodrich is in fact a semi-concentric castle, the great ditch to the south and east making a fully concentric plan impossible, though this natural defence was more than adequate compensation for additional man-made fortifications. Altogether it represented a formidable obstacle to any enemy.

Goodrich was the last castle in Herefordshire to hold out for Charles I in the Civil War, falling in 1646 to the assault of a locally made cannon known as Roaring Meg. Having breached the walls, Meg was taken off in triumph and preserved on Castle Green in Hereford, where it still stands. Some of the 10-kilo (200-pound) cannon balls with which it smashed the stonework are in the castle grounds.

The Norman keep from the inner courtyard. On the first floor is the original main doorway, its piers and wide arch framing a later, Gothic window. To the right is the great hall.

This was the last time Goodrich played any part in Britain's history. It gradually decayed into what Wordsworth regarded as, 'the noblest ruin in Herefordshire'. He was a regular visitor to these parts, and in 1828 took particular offence at a vast mock Gothic castle which Sir Samuel Meyrick, a wealthy local antiquary, built half a mile away from Goodrich. He was so incensed at this intrusion into the view that he said he, 'could almost have wished for the power to blow away Sir Samuel's impertinent structure and all the possessions it contained'. He would, therefore, be glad that the house has now been demolished and shipped stone by stone to the United States. Now the view is much as it was before the intrusion, and not very different from that surveyed by William de Valence and his attendants when they created this dominating castle on the rock above the Wye, guarding England against invasion from over the border.

ABOVE Goodrich as it might have looked in the early fourteenth century. William de Valence, uncle of Edward I, had completed it about thirty years before and the heavily fortified barbican had recently been added, providing an initial and highly efficient deterrent to any attacker.

TOP Looking down on the Wye from Goodrich, as its first defenders must have done seven centuries ago. From its crag the castle commanded both an ancient crossing of the river and the old Roman road from Gloucester to Caerleon.

# KENILWORTH CASTLE

## WARWICKSHIRE

T HE BED of the lake is but a rushy swamp; and the massive ruins of the castle only serve to show what their splendour once was and to impress on the musing visitor the transitory values of human possessions and the happiness of those who enjoy a humble lot in virtuous contentment.

Thus wrote Sir Walter Scott in *Kenilworth*, the novel which was inspired by the castle and which in turn inspired a new interest in what has been called 'the grandest fortress ruin in England'.

Scott's interest in Kenilworth was certainly justified both by its history and by its grandeur. In the seventeenth century Sir William Dugdale, the famous antiquary, reckoned that it 'ranked in third place, at least, with the most stately castles of England'. He counted it 'the glory of these parts'. Over 400 years before, it had been reckoned so important that it was one of the four castles that the barons required King John to deliver to them as sureties of his good faith over Magna Carta. There could have been no more impressive indication that Kenilworth was indeed reckoned to be the foremost fortress in the Midlands.

Part of the royal manor of Stoneleigh at the time of *Domesday*, the Kenilworth estates were granted

by Henry I to his Chamberlain, Geoffrey de Clinton, in the early years of the twelfth century. Geoffrey built a simple motte-and-bailey castle with a timber superstructure, and around 1160 the great square stone keep which still bears the family name was built by Geoffrey's son.

The castle was garrisoned for Henry II at the time of the rebellion in 1173, and he was so impressed by its strength and importance that he sequestered it, compensating the Clintons with estates in Buckinghamshire. Henry and his successors, King John and Henry III, all spent significant sums on enlarging the castle and

improving its defences. John built a curtain wall, but it was Henry III who made it one of the strongest fortresses in the land. Although a bad statesman, he was a considerable strategist and he recognized that the best form of defence, other than a natural precipice, was water. He therefore created a lake around Kenilworth by damming a series of streams flowing through the valley. He also erected two more lines of moats on the north side, the only one not protected by lake water. In all, the water defences covered more than 40 hectares (100 acres), vastly more than those at Caerphilly.

The romantic ruins of Kenilworth. To the far left is the gatehouse, with the barn to its right, both built by Robert Dudley, Earl of Leicester. In the centre is the Norman keep. Facing the lower corner of the curtain wall is John of Gaunt's great hall, and beyond, to the right, is the range known as Leicester's Buildings. It was in Leicester's time that the formal gardens were laid out.

Defences like these were specifically designed to keep siege engines at bay and they were soon put to the test. For Henry III gave Kenilworth to his sister Eleanor and her husband, Simon de Montfort, the man who was to become his sworn enemy. It was from Kenilworth that Simon organized his revolt against the king, and for a time the king's son, the Lord Edward, and the king's brother were imprisoned there. After the battle of Evesham in 1265, at which de Montfort was killed, his son, another Simon, rallied his supporters at Kenilworth and the king's son lay siege. It was a longer and even more bitter siege than that at Rochester fifty years before. Unlike Rochester, Kenilworth was impervious to mining because of its water defences, and the attack was concentrated on the one

The keep from the south-west, built around 1160 and adapted by Lord Leicester four hundred years later to the needs of a more peaceful age.

side not protected by the lake. Great siege engines were set up, and wooden towers, known as belfries or bears, one large enough to contain two hundred archers, were constructed. Those

Leicester's Building, built towards the end of the castle's active life, in the late sixteenth century. In the background is the great hall.

besieged returned the fire in good measure, and there are contemporary accounts of boulders colliding in mid-air as bombardment and counter bombardment raged. The king himself was at Kenilworth from 23 June until 16 December 1266 directing the siege operations. At one stage the Archbishop of Canterbury was produced before the castle to excom-

municate those inside. We are told that the defenders mocked this attempt at moral pressure by dressing a figure in a monk's habit and getting him to pronounce a similar sentence on the Archbishop.

The king's forces offered terms to the defenders, known as the Dictum of Kenilworth. This allowed them to regain the lands on payment of a fine,

but the terms were not accepted immediately and the siege went on, the defenders hoping for relief. It did not come, and the garrison finally surrendered in December, on terms which allowed them to evacuate the castle with honour, because they were starving and an epidemic had broken out. This protracted siege proved the effectiveness of the water defences and

was the most famous moment in the castle's history.

Kenilworth, however, did not sink into obscurity thereafter. In 1279 Roger de Mortimer held a tournament on the dam of the lake, and for three days a hundred knights tilted before a hundred ladies. It was at Kenilworth in 1327 that Edward II was told of his deposition and forced to abdicate, and in 1376 the castle came into the possession of Blanche, wife of John of Gaunt. He did much to improve its comforts, adding the great hall and a long wing of sumptuous private apartments.

It remained a royal residence for another two hundred years, until in 1563 Elizabeth I bestowed it on her favourite, Robert Dudley, Earl of Leicester. He further extended and 'improved' it. There was no longer any need for massive defences, and he so modernized the keep that, we are told, he made a mockery of its massive strength. In 1575 he entertained Elizabeth for nineteen days of elaborate dances, plays and 'medieval' jousting, and water pageants using the lake, as John of Gaunt had done before him, as a splendid facility for enjoyment. It is said that the pageantry cost him £1,000 a day and

ABOVE Jousting before ladies, as Roger de Mortimer's knights did at Kenilworth, at the famous tournament on the dam on the lake in 1279.

BELOW Robert Dudley spent a fortune on turning Kenilworth into a palace to suit his queen's desire for comfort, and on extravagances of all kinds to entertain her. In this contemporary painting of them dancing together Elizabeth appears to be literally transported.

ABOVE John of Gaunt's great hall, a beautiful building with fine lancet windows, some of which still have their original stone mullions and transoms.

that he spent £100,000 in providing accommodation for the queen and her court. It was Dudley who built the great gatehouse to the north, the range of buildings still known as Leicester's Buildings, and the long barn. Leicester was the last of the great Lords of Kenilworth. At his death the castle was neglected, and although it changed hands during the Civil War there was no real fighting here. Major Hawkesworth, the Parliamentary Commander at Warwick, acquired the estate and converted Leicester's gatehouse into a private house. Parliament ordered the demolition of the castle in 1649 and the orders were carried out in part, the north wall of the keep and the north curtain wall being destroyed shortly afterwards.

After the Restoration the castle passed first to the daughters of the Earl of Monmouth, then to the Earl of Rochester and finally to the Earl of Clarendon. A noble ruin, it remained in

Lord Leicester's gatehouse – the only part of the castle to remain habitable.

his family until it was bought in 1937 by Sir John Davenport Siddely and given to the nation.

Today only Leicester's gatehouse remains habitable – the local council has its chamber there. The ruin, however, is indeed a noble one and, although the keep is without the upper part of its turrets, it is clear just how impressive it must have been when it rose 30 metres (100 feet) or more. We can see too the remains of John of Gaunt's palatial great hall, which must in its day have rivalled the great hall at Westminster. The water defences have now gone, but the bailey wall on the west, south and east sides is well preserved, as are two of its three towers, although the third, the Swan Tower, is in ruins. So is the original main entrance, the rectangular gate-tower to which a double-towered gatehouse was added in the thirteenth century. Enough remains, however, for us to visualize some of the drama and pageantry of Kenilworth's past, enough to make those with imagination understand why this great ruined medieval fortress so inspired Sir Walter Scott.

# 4 FORTIFIED MANOR

THE GREAT NORMAN AND EDWARDIAN castles were essentially military strongholds, where creature comforts took a definite second place to military needs. Medieval kings and great barons were constantly on the move. Where the king was the court was, and the royal progress was one means of keeping control of the kingdom, and of keeping in touch with its various parts in an age when man could only travel as quickly as the fastest horse could take him. So it was with the nobility : there are many colourful accounts of the great baggage trains of feudal lords on the move from estate to estate in the centuries before the fixed abode, the country seat, became the normal focus of noble life.

During the long reign of Edward III (1327–77) things began to change. The king himself, like the great Edward I, his grandfather, was a compulsive builder. But his building schemes laid as much emphasis on splendour and comfort as they did on strong defence. Ably assisted by one of the greatest royal servants of the Middle Ages, William of Wykeham (who rose from royal kennel keeper to Lord Chancellor and Bishop of Winchester), Edward spent lavishly on building. He scoured the country for labourers and even had a press gang system to compel people to work for him. He once had his labourers dressed in red so that they would be instantly recognizable if they tried to get away. After the Black Death of 1348, which reduced the population by a third, there was many a squabble over wage rates : the labourer was in a seller's market, and the clergy and nobility were as demanding of the services of builders and craftsmen as was the king.

Unfortunately little of Edward's work has survived. Nothing but a few mounds remain of the great castle he built at Queenborough to command one of the chief sea routes to the Thames, between the Isle of Sheppey and the mainland. Nor is there much outward sign of the splendidly fortified and rebuilt Windsor Castle for which Edward was responsible and where, in a magnificent timbered hall, the first ceremonies of his noble Order of the Garter were held. Altogether Edward's buildings at Windsor cost £50,000 and were by far the most expensive public works of the Middle Ages. And yet at the same time as he was transforming the Conqueror's Thames-side fortress he was spending some £30,000 at Westminster and over £1,000 a year on the fortifications at Calais.

Calais was of enormous importance to Edward, but his political adventures in France were responsible for much private castle building in Britain towards the end of his reign. For Edward lost command of the seas for a time. In 1377 the French actually landed and sacked Rye and Winchelsea. This threat provoked the first of those invasion scares which punctuated English history through the time of the Armada and the Napoleonic Wars and on to Hitler and Operation Sealion in 1940. It inevitably led to an improvement of defences along and near the coast. Castles at Rochester, Southampton and Porchester were all modernized, and even the great Edwardian castles in Wales received attention.

# HOUSES

Herstmonceux, a splendid example of a moated and crenellated manor, was built of Flemish brick in the mid-fifteenth century by Roger de Fiennes, Treasurer of the King's Household. Its gatehouse, completely restored earlier this century, is 25·5 metres (84 feet) high, with a fine arched bridge spanning the moat. The castle now houses the Royal Observatory.

RIGHT The great tower of Caister, the 'water castle' built by Sir John Fastolf in 1431. Despite the machicolations, the large windows in the tower and in the great hall to the right denote that a desire for comfort equalled the need for security.

However, it is the private rather than the royal castles of the fourteenth and fifteenth centuries that are of most interest. The French threat persuaded the king and his weak (and eventually deposed) successor Richard II (1377–99) to issue a number of licences to wealthy subjects to fortify, or crenellate, their manors or to build castles as their country homes. Scotney Castle in Kent is an early example. It has been much altered over the centuries and only a fragment of the original castle remains, but it was once a fairly formidable deterrent with a moat around two islands, one of which was heavily fortified and contained four corner towers. The second island was rather like the barbican of many earlier medieval fortresses, an outer enclosure with its gate lying beyond the main defences and encircled by its own ditch.

The finest of the fourteenth-century fortified manor houses to survive in anything like its original state is Penshurst, also in Kent. Penshurst has no moat and originally had no significant defences either. It was one of the earliest country mansions to be built for a successful merchant rather than for a nobleman. Sir John de Pulteney, who was four times Lord Mayor of London, was a wealthy draper. Because of the French scare he was given a licence to crenellate and Penshurst became one of the first fortified manor houses. It never became a proper fortress, however, nor was the comfort of its interior sacrificed in any way.

A combination of strength and comfort was the hallmark of the later medieval castle or fortified manor. The appearance of strength was often in itself as much an expression and symbol of the owner's grandeur as a reflection of military need. But although it was only in the south that there was a remote danger of foreign invasion, throughout the country there was a genuine need for proper protection, particularly in the lifetimes of those weak kings Richard II and Henry VI, during whose reign (1422–61), and for twenty years after, that series of civil wars known as the 'Wars of the Roses' raged.

The late fourteenth century and most of the fifteenth were characterized by a form of fragmented or bastard feudalism. The presence of a weak king on the throne allowed powerful magnates both to become tyrants in their own territories and to invade their neighbours' land. These baronial gangsters, whose activities were reminiscent of the anarchy of Stephen's reign in the twelfth century, had a powerful influence on the architecture of the time. For one thing, it was necessary for men of substance to have adequate protection against the attacks of marauding gangs. For another, these robber barons themselves could never be entirely sure of the loyalties of the mercenaries whom they employed. That is why, within many castles, they adapted or built their own quarters, entirely selfcontained and separate from those of the military retainers they employed. We can see examples of these special, and often highly luxurious, quarters at Richmond in Yorkshire, at Ludlow, at Warwick – where two towers were reserved for the lord and his family – and at Raglan where the lord's Yellow Tower was in effect a castle in its own right.

One of the most interesting castles of this period, because it is perhaps the best documented, is Caister Castle in Norfolk. It was built by Sir John Fastolf, who acquired a vast fortune as a result of his prowess on the battlefields of France. The inventory taken at his death in 1469 gives an idea of the sort of sumptuous comfort in which military success enabled him to live. He had silver and silver gilt weighing nearly 1,500 oz as well as 98 oz of gold articles, and he could supply from his own resources silver dishes for a banquet of over a hundred people, and had 900 litres (200 gallons) of wine in his cellar.

Caister Castle passed into the hands of the Pastons, a Norfolk family whose letters and personal papers have miraculously survived. They give a unique picture of rural life in fifteenth-century England. In one of her letters Margaret Paston describes the sort of attack to which a country house of the period could well be subjected. No passage better illustrates why manor houses had to have adequate defences. She tells us how a thousand people had arrived at one of the family manors at Gresham :

Arrayd in manner of war, with cuirasses, coats of mail, steel helmets, glaives [swords], bows, arrows, large, shields, guns, pans with fire, long cromes [poles] to draw down houses, ladders, and picks with which they mined down the walls and long trees with which they broke down gates and doors, and so came into the said mansion,

the wife of your beseecher at that time being therein, and twelve persons with her – the which persons they drove out of the said mansions and mined down the walls of the chamber wherein the wife of your said beseecher was, and bear her out of the gates and cut asunder the posts of the houses and let them fall, and broke up all the chambers and coffers of the said mansion, and rifled and bear away stuff, array and money to the value of £200.

This was in Norfolk. But such incidents were by no means unusual, and no properties were immune from attack. Particularly vulnerable were the clergy who, because the Pope was reckoned to be a French puppet (for seventy years he was obliged to reside at Avignon in southern France), were especially unpopular. During the fourteenth century three senior bishops were brutally murdered,

The newel staircase in the keep at Tattershall Castle. The keep is perhaps the finest brick building in the whole of England. Built by Ralph Cromwell in the fifteenth century, it was bought and restored, like Bodiam, by Lord Curzon in the twentieth.

one being dragged from his London home and murdered by the mob outside. As a result many bishops' palaces became especially strong fortified manors and one, at Wells, still survives surrounded by its moat, today a beautiful and peaceful reminder of earlier troubles.

Abbeys, too, often needed some form of defence : in 1382, a year after the Peasants Revolt, one of the earliest and finest brick buildings in England was erected at Thornton Abbey in Lincolnshire in the form of a splendid defensive gatehouse. Brick was increasingly used for dwellings that were designed

LEFT A gunner's eye view through a keyhole gunport, showing how the gunports in this and the neighbouring tower cover the intervening ditch.

ABOVE A gunner using a barrel-forged and breech-loading cannon in a keyhole gunport adapted from an arrow slit. The gunner's mate is preparing a red-hot wire to fire the cannon, which is firmly clamped to a wooden bed.

RIGHT A breech-loading gun of 1460–70. The gun is loaded by knocking out the wedge, allowing the chamber to be removed. When loaded, the chamber is replaced in the breech-piece and the wedge driven home, forcing the chamber hard up against the barrel.

not so much to play a part in a major war as to deter medieval hooligans. The two finest of all brick castles are Herstmonceux in Sussex and Tattershall in Lincolnshire. They are really crenellated mansions, early country seats.

One final thing about the fourteenth century must be mentioned – the coming of the gun and cannon. Gunpowder was first used to discharge missiles in the fourteenth century, but guns and cannons were not widely used until a century later. Initially they made little difference to siege warfare. Some of the fortified manor houses already referred to had cannon slits, but attackers found heavy and cumbersome iron guns particularly difficult to manoeuvre. As early as 1405, however, Henry VI was able to show just what could be done by a warrior who had the cash and manpower to handle a heavy siege train when he reduced the Percy strongholds of Alnwick, Berwick and Warkworth in Northumberland in double-quick time.

The Wars of the Roses were wars determined on the battlefield rather than by siege. Castles did not play the significant part that they had done during the troubles of Stephen's reign. And although in places as far apart and as different as Oxburgh in Norfolk, Baddesley in Warwickshire, Stokesay on the Shropshire border and Hever in Kent, country gentlemen and noblemen continued to live in fortified dwellings, the emphasis was increasingly on comfort. Some castles and manor houses were indeed to play their part in a later civil war but the only true fortresses to be built in Britain after this time were the coastal defences of Henry VIII.

# BODIAM CASTLE

## Sussex

EEN FROM the south-east, Bodiam, set in parkland and mirrored in the still waters of its moat, has a rare grace and beauty, qualities we do not normally associate with massive fortifications. And yet, though Bodiam had apartments of true elegance and splendour, it was far more a castle than a fortified manor. It would have been difficult for any fourteenth-century attacker to overcome the determined defender without great effort and considerable risk.

That rare thing among castles, a private fortress built with royal permission to deter the king's enemies, we owe Bodiam to the vulnerability of southern England towards the end of the fourteenth century. For about fifteen years the command of the Channel was very much in French hands, and in 1377 they sacked Rye, Yarmouth and Newport. It was in this atmosphere of alarm that on 21 October 1385 Richard II gave Sir Edward Dalyngrigge a licence, 'that he may strengthen with a wall of stone and lime and crenellate, and may construct and make into a castle his manor house at Bodyham, near the sea, in the County of Sussex, for the defences of the adjacent County and the resistance of our enemies.'

Sir Edward, who was well known at court and a veteran of Edward III's wars, decided to interpret the licence very liberally. He abandoned his

Only Leeds Castle rivals Bodiam in the romantic beauty of its setting, yet it is clear that any invading French force, against whose threat it was built, would have found it a formidable enough fortress at the end of the fourteenth century.

existing manor house, and on a new site nearby, halfway up the slope of a hill, built one of the last medieval castles in Britain. It commanded the valley of the Rother, which was navigable up to Bodiam bridge and regarded as part of the port of Winchelsea, itself sacked in only 1380.

Sir Edward never had cause to use his castle and in the six hundred years since he built it it has been attacked only twice, and on each occasion easily taken. In 1483 it was captured by the Earl of Surrey for Richard III after its owner, Sir Thomas Lewknor, had incurred the king's displeasure. Sir Thomas seems to have put up barely token resistance. Parliamentary for-

ces took it with equal ease in 1643, probably because the owner, the Earl of Thanet, was not in residence at the time. The interior of the castle was severely damaged by the Parliamentarians, but contenting themselves with that destruction they left the exterior virtually unmolested.

It remained a picturesque ruin until

the beginning of the twentieth century when Lord Curzon, former Viceroy of India, bought it, restored it with meticulous care and scholarship and gave it to the National Trust. Thanks to Lord Curzon we can today see Bodiam from the outside much as Sir Edward Dalyngrigge left it. We can appreciate the architectural 'purity' of the building for it was completed within a very few years and never subsequently altered. Although the interior apartments are in ruins, enough remains for us to envisage what they were like in the late

Soft greys and golds of limestone towers reflected in the lake add an air of mystery to Bodiam's seclusion.

ABOVE The south-east tower and part of the ruined hall. The walls are crenellated and lined with deep embrasures from which to fire across the moat, but the generous windows are a sign of the changing times.

OPPOSITE The vaulting in the cylindrical corner towers has collapsed, but the arches that supported the ribs remain. Holes in the wall indicate the slots for beams to hold the upper floor.

fourteenth century.

Bodiam's plan is a very simple one. Curtain walls, two storeys high, enclose a rectangular court. There are four drum-shaped corner towers rising to a height of 18·2 metres (60 feet). There is a square tower on each flank, an impressive twin-towered gatehouse in the centre of the north front and a postern tower opposite it in the centre of the south front. The whole is set in an artificial lake, some 152 metres by 107 metres (500 feet by 350 feet) and fed from the nearby River Rother. Today the castle is approached by a

straight causeway over the moat, a recent replacement of a sixteenth-century one. The approach designed by Sir Edward was a much more complicated one, calculated to expose any attacker and give the maximum opportunity to the defenders. For to approach the main entrance meant crossing from the west bank to the octagonal island in the moat and turning right through a barbican, beyond which was the main entrance to the castle. There were three draw-

bridges to negotiate, and all the time the attacker would be vulnerable to fire from the castle walls. Even the approach to the postern involved crossing two drawbridges, one at each end of the original wooden bridge across the moat.

Traces of this elaborate system were uncovered when Lord Curzon drained the lake during his restoration. Although the barbican has gone, the other castle defences remain, including one of the original portcullises

made of iron-studded oak. We can see too the murder holes above the vaulted passages of the main gateway and the postern. A particularly interesting feature of a castle built at the beginning of a new era of warfare are the arrow slits adapted for guns by the insertion of port holes beneath – not that any guns used at Bodiam would have been of great deterrent value.

Although the inner buildings have been destroyed, we can appreciate something of the elegance of chapel and residence from the ruins. We know that the walls facing on to the courtyard were generously fitted with windows to afford the maximum light to the apartments, and we know too that comfort and sanitation were not neglected. Lord Curzon counted thirty-three fireplaces, and twenty-eight lavatories which were built into the walls and discharged into the moat.

Bodiam was built at a time when the lord of a castle had to depend increasingly on hired mercenaries rather than feudal retainers, and the new element of danger this introduced into domestic relationships was clearly recognized here. There are no connecting doors and passages between the owner's quarters and the 'retainers''. The retainers' hall and kitchen are next to each other, but no servant could get from either to any other part of the castle without venturing into the courtyard. There his movements could be observed from the gatehouse which, like the well in the south-west tower, was under the owner's control.

Everything at Bodiam was arranged with similar careful thought. It is one of the most compact and convenient of fortified dwellings, and in spite of the destruction it is still easy to visualize this as a dwelling fortified of necessity, but 'all comfortable within'.

OPPOSITE The symmetrical plan of this courtyard castle, with its sixteenth-century causeway and rectangular moat, can be clearly seen from the air.

BELOW The elegant screen passage at the end of the lord's hall.

# HEVER CASTLE

## KENT

THERE IS probably no important house in England that has been more restored in the present century than Hever. Its associations with Henry VIII and Anne Boleyn give it a perpetual fascination. Its contents, garden and adjacent village make it a major tourist attraction, but enough of the original castle remains, and the restoration has been sufficiently authentic, for it to be well worthy of inclusion in any chapter on fortified manor houses. For that is precisely what Hever, in spite of its name, was. Its massive gatehouse and sturdy walls were sufficient to protect its inhabitants from the activities of marauding bands and deter any gangs of anarchic ne'er-do-wells, but it could never have withstood sustained attack by even medieval cannon.

Hever dates from the time when disturbers of the civil peace were active in rural England. In the century before the Battle of Bosworth in 1485, when Henry VII came to the throne and general peace broke out, Englishmen with possessions to defend needed houses from which they could defend them ; so it was that the first licence to crenellate Hever was granted around 1340. Precisely what was done by William de Hever to fortify the house at the time is uncertain, but in 1384, by which time the castle had passed to Sir John de Cobham (who was responsible for much of the defences of Cooling Castle, also in Kent), the threat of the French invasion inspired the king to grant permission to crenellate fairly freely in the southern counties. Hever again received a licence. The embattled walls of the quadrangular house and the moat both date from this time.

Throughout the fifteenth century the defences were well maintained, no doubt to deter the aggressive intent of Kentish marauders like Lord Saye and Sele. In 1462 the castle was acquired by Sir Geoffrey Bullen, Lord Mayor of London in 1459 and a successful hatter in the City, and he was probably responsible for the massive three-storey gatehouse.

The Bullen family prospered, and Sir Geoffrey's grandson Thomas married into the high nobility. His wife, Lady Elizabeth Howard, was daughter of the Earl of Surrey, second Duke of Norfolk. Sir Thomas Bullen himself gained the favour of Henry VIII, was Ambassador to the Emperor Maximilian, acted as envoy to the Pope and, as Ambassador to France, was present at the Field of Cloth of Gold in 1520. In 1522 he was Treasurer of the Household and by 1523 a Knight of the Garter. Two years later he became Viscount Rochford and in 1529 Earl of Wiltshire and of Ormond.

Sir Thomas Boleyn (as he now called himself) owed much of his success to the favours granted by and to his daughters. The elder, Mary, was mistress to the king and the younger, Anne, succeeded her as lady-in-waiting to Catherine of Aragon – and to the king's bed. Catherine was now barren, Anne was attractive and the king was desperate for a son. There followed the royal divorce and the unending religious, political and social consequences of the breach with Rome and the Reformation.

Henry was a frequent visitor to Hever during this decisive period in England's history and the relatively modest manor house in Kent became one of the best known houses in the country. But its period of glory was brief. Though Henry married Anne in

It was Henry VIII who brought fame to Hever through his passion for Anne Boleyn. Here they are seen walking together in the long gallery on one of his frequent visits.

ABOVE Lord Astor's Hever, showing the vast mock Tudor village that he built to house his guests, and his elaborate ornamental gardens and 13-hectare (35-acre) lake. Bordering the lake is an Italian garden with pergolas, Roman baths, grottoes and marble pavements. The whole astonishing venture was undertaken in the early 1900s with an army of workmen, excavators, steam diggers and seven miles of railway line.

1533, by 1536, disappointed in her ability to produce a son and attracted by Anne's maid-of-honour, Jane Seymour, Henry had Anne arrested on a charge of High Treason and adultery with four men, including her own brother. The queen was be-headed. Within two years her father was dead and Henry had taken possession of Hever. In 1540 it featured in his marital adventures again for he

The dining hall. Elaborately restored by Lord Astor, it has an oak-panelled ceiling and a fine minstrels' gallery with a network of intricate carving. The tapestry is sixteenth-century Flemish. One of the door-locks here is said to have belonged to Henry VIII; he took it everywhere with him and used it to fasten his bedroom door.

The inner hall, richly panelled in Italian walnut. The columns are carved from a magnificent walnut tree from Caserta, which was cut down in 1747 and used for years as a winepress. The log then passed through three generations before being bought by a timber merchant in the 1890s, who finally sold it to Hever.

gave it as a consolation to his fourth wife, Anne of Cleves, whom he married for diplomatic reasons. He had admired Holbein's portrait of her but when she arrived he took an instant physical dislike to her and divorced her after six months. The house remained in her possession until her death in 1557, when Mary Tudor gave it to Sir Edward Waldegrave, one of her favourite courtiers.

Thereafter it passed by marriage or purchase through several families, and enjoyed more than three centuries of rural obscurity. By the nineteenth century it was a working farmhouse. Obscurity and neglect coincided and there was little attempt to alter or 'improve' Hever. So it was as a somewhat dilapidated but relatively unspoiled fortified manor house that Hever attracted the attentions and

The castle from the south-west. On the right is the imposing three-storey gatehouse, heavily defended against marauders.

affections of William Waldorf Astor, who purchased it in 1903.

Astor lavished money upon it, transforming it from a farmhouse to a mansion, filling it with artistic treasures and much splendid Edwardian woodwork and panelling. Expense was of no consequence, either in the house or outside. The gardens were laid out in the Italian style, with a riot of statuary and ornament. The farm buildings were converted into a Tudor village to house the servants and guests. In December 1904 there were 748 workmen engaged upon the castle, village and gardens. The excavation of the lake occupied the labours of another 800 men. To make room for the village, much more extensive in acreage than the house, the bed of the river was pushed back 100 yards to the north of its natural course. Chimney designs were copied from Hampton Court, and timber and oak salvaged from the Tudor stables, which had stood in front of the house since the early sixteenth century, were used in the construction of the village.

It has to be said though that the result appeared remarkably authentic. The village, with its assortment of roofs, gables and chimneys, looks as if it could indeed have been preserved in some architectural amber through the centuries.

Within the castle itself much of the original fabric was preserved and the restoration done with meticulous care. The contents were amassed at vast expense, but without the expert knowledge that would have guaranteed authenticity. As an example of the wealth of the twentieth century 'rescuing and glorifying' a building of the fourteenth and fifteenth centuries, Hever is notable. It makes a marked and fascinating contrast to Stokesay, a fortified manor house of an earlier period, to Bodiam, more castle than manor house, and to Leeds, a castle early transformed into a sumptuous and stately home. Unfortunately the enormous cost of maintaining Hever forced the present Lord Astor, in 1982, to put it on the market.

# LEEDS CASTLE
## KENT

UNTIL RECENTLY an elegant private country house, Leeds Castle today is the headquarters of a charitable trust to which it was bequeathed. It is a living and a peaceful place. It owes its transition from castle through fortified manor to country house, and its survival from ruination, largely to the grace and beauty of its setting, a setting which so delighted and inspired successive owners that Leeds has become what one historian of European castles called 'the loveliest castle in the world'.

Where visitors now catch their breath at the beauty of this Kentish castle reflected in its lake, and where scholars now work in the cause of science, warriors once fought and successive queens of England took their ease and, over the centuries, transformed a fortress into a palace.

The strategic importance and defensive possibilities of this site on the River Len, where the river broadens to surround two small islands, was first appreciated by Ledian or Leede, chief minister and courtier of Ethelbert IV of Kent. Here, in the middle of the ninth century, he built a wooden castle.

After the Conquest William granted Leede's Manor to Hamon de Crèvecoeur, one of his courtiers, and it was Hamon's son, Robert, who first built a stone castle here, consisting of a keep and gatehouse. Almost nothing of this first stone castle survives, save a cellar and some masonry from the castle's oldest tower, the Gloriette.

During the Civil War of King Stephen's reign, when the Empress Matilda, daughter of Henry I and wife of the Count of Anjou, invaded England and disputed for the throne, the Earl of Gloucester, Matilda's bastard brother, briefly held Leeds for his sister before it fell to Stephen. However, the castle remained in the hands of the Crèvecoeurs until, in the turmoil of Henry III's reign, another Robert (great grandson of the first builder) took arms with Simon de Montfort and was dispossessed of the castle. Henry III then gave Leeds to Roger de Leyburn, whom he made Sheriff of Kent and Warden of the Cinque Ports. Roger died while accompanying Prince Edward, later Edward I, to the Holy Land, and it was Roger's son, William de Leyburn, another notable medieval warrior, who, in 1278, conveyed the castle, 'to the august Prince and my most dear Lord Edward, noble King of England, and my fair Lady Eleanor, Queen of England'.

Edward and Eleanor obviously had a high affection for Leeds. They spent much time here and considerably improved and extended the castle, strengthening the curtain wall and building a new gatehouse and a chapel in the Gloriette, a chapel which was reconsecrated as a Chapel Royal by the Archbishop of Canterbury in May 1978. It was in this chapel that Edward ordered prayers to be said for the soul of Eleanor after her death in 1290. Unusual in medieval royal marriages, this was a marriage of love, and Edward was so distraught by the death of his dear queen that he ordered a cross to be erected at every town where her body rested on the way to Westminster – hence the many

The islands in the River Len proved a suitable situation for a castle as long ago as the ninth century, but the potential of the site was fully exploited when the river was flooded in the fourteenth century to form an artificial lake.

Eleanor Crosses, as at Banbury, and hence the name Charing Cross, where the most famous of them all was built for the *'Chère Reine'* (Dear Queen). In the chantry chapel at Leeds four canons and a clerk daily celebrated Mass for Eleanor's soul, and the chantry was confirmed by Edward II, Richard II, Henry VI and Henry VII 'forever'. But the king could not remain a widower forever, and in 1299 Edward I married Margaret of France at Canterbury, spent his honeymoon at Leeds and gave the castle to her, as he had given it to Eleanor. Thus it was that Leeds first became known as the Dower Castle or Ladies Castle.

Edward II was later to present the castle to one of his nobles, 'the rich Lord Bartholomew de Baldesmere', but his queen, Isabella, the 'She Wolf of France', was so incensed when Baldesmere's castellan refused to give her shelter in Leeds in 1321 that she forced the king to deal with this rebellious baron. Leeds was laid siege, the castle was captured and both Baldesmere and his castellan were beheaded. After Isabella had disposed of her husband in 1327 she took Leeds for herself and held it until her enforced retirement to Castle Rising.

By now the castle had extensive water defences. They had been created, like those at Kenilworth and Caerphilly, by damming the river to form an artificial lake. Leeds was thus an extensive and significantly fortified castle, and after Isabella's departure

Leeds, the most romantic castle in England.

Edward III further strengthened and extended it as well as redecorating the royal chambers in the Gloriette.

Richard II regarded Leeds so highly that he commissioned the famous Henry Yevele, who built the great nave at Canterbury and re-fashioned Westminster Hall, to carry out improvements. He also gave it to his queen, Anne of Bohemia, and used the castle much himself after her death.

After Richard's deposition and murder, Henry Bolingbroke, now Henry IV, and his second wife, Joan of Navarre, retreated to Leeds from London during the plague of 1403. The castle was given to Queen Joan, but after the king's death she was charged with witchcraft and confined in Pevensey Castle, her goods forfeit. Although she had a reputation for sorcery, it is very probable that these charges were instigated by her stepson, Henry V, who wanted to give Leeds to his new queen, Catherine de Valois, the 'fair Kate' of Shakespeare's *Henry V*. Joan was released before Henry's death in 1422 but Kate remained at Leeds, and it was here that she fell in love with Owen Tudor, clerk of her wardrobe. They married secretly and when their liaison was discovered they were both imprisoned, though the queen was released and Owen subsequently escaped from the Tower. It was their son, Edmund, Earl of Richmond, who became the father of Henry VII and thus the founder of the Tudor dynasty.

Catherine was the last queen to own Leeds, but Henry VIII took a great liking to the castle and spent freely on enlarging and beautifying it. He completed the transformation from fortress to palace, though he retained the castle's defences, mindful of that threat of invasion which caused him to build his great chain of coastal forts. It was Henry who let the light into the castle, adding a storey to the Gloriette

Leeds in daffodil time. Reaching out over the water is the oldest part of the castle, the tower known as the Gloriette, to which Henry VIII added the top storey.

and putting in large windows in the royal apartments. He also built the Maiden's Tower to house the maids-of-honour. It is very probable that Anne Boleyn spent some time here when she was in waiting to Catherine of Aragon.

Although he valued, extended and used Leeds, Henry VIII was in fact the last royal owner, for he bestowed the castle on Sir Anthony St Leger for his services as Lord Deputy in Ireland. It was sadly lost to the St Legers when one of Sir Anthony's descendants suffered financial ruin by backing Raleigh's ill-fated expedition in search of Eldorado. Leeds then passed through the hands of two Kentish families until it became the property of John Culpeper, Charles I's Chancellor of the Exchequer. The most loyal of the king's servants, his devotion was rewarded after the Restoration by Charles II, who restored the castle to him and gave him enormous tracts of land in Virginia as well. Leeds and the American estates descended through the female line to the family

of Lord Fairfax. Robert Fairfax entertained George III here in 1778. After his death the castle passed through marriage into the Wickham Martin family in whose possession it remained until, in 1926, it was bought by Olive, Lady Baillie.

In the eighteenth century it had been much 'improved' in the Gothic manner and it was further medievalized in the nineteenth century. Lady Baillie restored it still more and created here a gracious home in which

RIGHT When the royal maids-of-honour waited on their queen at Leeds in the early sixteenth century, they would have slept here, in the maid-of-honour's bedroom, and it is likely that Anne Boleyn would have used the room when she was in attendance on Catherine of Aragon. The Flemish tapestry and oak furniture are contemporary with the transformation of the castle from fortress to palace.

BELOW The view across the moat from the large casement windows installed by Henry VIII in the Gloriette.

she entertained some of the most notable figures of the inter-war years. On her death in 1974 she left it in trust for the nation, anxious that people should be able to enjoy its beauty and also that it should be a centre for study and discussion, especially for the interchange of information by those engaged in medical research.

Because it has remained in continuous occupation, and because succes-

LEFT The banqueting hall, 23 metres (75 feet) long, runs between the chapel and the gallery along the west side of the castle. Its bow window dates from the rebuilding by Henry VIII in 1512, and the vast refectory table, cut from a single oak plank, is seventeenth century. On the far wall is a Flemish tapestry of the 1490s portraying the Adoration of the Magi. Tapestries woven before 1500 are rare and this is an unusually beautiful example. The floor, of double-dovetailed ebony, was laid by Lady Baillie in the 1920s.

sive generations felt the need to adapt and improve it to maintain its comfort as a home, Leeds has none of the 'authentic' appearance of the partially ruined Bodiam or Caerphilly, or of the many other deserted castles described in this book. It may be idle to pretend that it looks like a stern fortress, but it is possible nonetheless to trace its medieval defences and to appreciate that what has been changed and domesticated once had a very real military purpose. Today the atmosphere of Leeds is certainly one of serene calm and beauty, and its rooms full of treasures and fine furnishings make it a very stately home.

BELOW The queen's bedroom, next to the banqueting hall. The oak furniture includes a splendid four-poster bed and a medieval wall cupboard known as an aumbry, used originally to store sacred vessels in a church. The carved oak-beamed ceiling is particularly fine.

# STOKESAY CASTLE

## SHROPSHIRE

TOKESAY is not really a castle at all : it is the best preserved and least altered fortified manor house in England. Lying in a lush and tranquil Shropshire valley, it has today an air of quiet and gentle domesticity about it. But its fortifications were not erected for show. Stokesay dates from the thirteenth century, when this part of the country, the turbulent Welsh Marches, was far from peaceful. A man needed to take more than token precautions to protect his possessions and those who worked on his manor.

The name Stokesay derives from the 'stoke' or dairy farm given by one of the Conqueror's followers at the beginning of the twelfth century to Theodoric de Say from Clun. It was in about 1240 that one of the Says built the two lower storeys of the present north tower, the oldest surviving part of Stokesay. In 1280 Stokesay was bought by Laurence de Ludlow, a rich wool merchant, and some ten years later Edward I, conscious of the increasing vulnerability of the Marches, gave him a licence to crenellate. Laurence transformed Stokesay. He pulled down the existing wooden buildings, and before he died had built the high tower on the west front and the great hall, and had surrounded his manor with a moat and a curtain wall. He also added the present top storey to the north tower. It was in these imposing buildings that the rich and aspiring merchant entertained the Bishop of Hereford and his retinue for ten days in 1290.

Stokesay, from the churchyard. Evening sunlight and a profusion of ox-eye daisies enhance the gentle charm of this small secluded manor house.

Stokesay remained in the Ludlow family for three hundred years. It was then sold and resold until it became the property of Lord Craven, a fervent Royalist, who garrisoned it during the Civil War as an outpost of nearby Ludlow Castle, a key Royalist stronghold. Stokesay, however, suffered less than most of Charles I's fortifications, for in 1645 it surrendered to the Parliamentary forces without a struggle and was only nominally slighted.

After the Civil War the Cravens leased Stokesay to another neighbouring family who, from the early eighteenth century, in turn sub-let to a succession of local farmers. As a result it was sadly neglected. At one time the great hall was used as a cooper's

BELOW The beautiful great hall is the finest surviving example in England of a domestic hall of the thirteenth century. The splendid roof has been restored but many of the beams are original, their timbers blackened over the years by the smoke of open fires.

The timbered and finely carved seventeenth-century gatehouse into the courtyard.

(barrel-maker's) workshop and the solar became a granary. It was described as 'miserably neglected' when the Lord Craven of the day put urgent repairs in hand in the 1860s and in 1869 it was bought by John Hallcroft, Member of Parliament for Worcester, who saw it as his mission to restore and preserve the building. It has remained in the family ever since, carefully maintained but never fully inhabited.

Many of those buildings which the Bishop of Hereford must have admired in 1290 have gone. Enough remains, however, to give us a clear idea of what a moated and fortified manor house of the thirteenth century looked like, and because, for three centuries or more, it has been no family's major home, Stokesay has escaped the zeal of the improvers. The newest building on the site is the fine timbered gatehouse built around the turn of the seventeenth century. This gatehouse, elaborately decorated

Overlooking the hall, and adjoining it on the south side, is the solar. A magnificent carved overmantle crowns the fireplace, which is flanked by two 'squints', openings in the wall through which the lord and his family could watch the activity below.

with magnificent carvings of Adam and Eve with the serpent and the forbidden fruit, is the one part of Stokesay that is still a home. Very little of the curtain wall which Laurence began when he received his royal licence in 1291 remains, but there is enough to show that it was several feet thick and reached a height of 10·3 metres (34 feet) from the bottom of the moat. It was certainly a very effective and obvious deterrent against any marauding band intent on plundering the rich merchant's house.

At Stokesay we can imagine how any lord of the manor would have entertained his guests and tenants. The best evidence of Laurence's wealth is the great hall, begun in about 1285. Probably the finest example we have of the hall of a medieval house, it is 10·3 metres (34 feet) high, 9·5 metres (31 feet) wide and 15·8 metres (52 feet) long. There is eloquent evidence of the open stone hearth in the blackened timbers of the roof above. The roof was originally

supported by three massive 'crucks', parts of which still rest on stone pilasters on the hall walls. Stokesay was one of the first houses to have glazed windows. Glass was so rare and expensive in the thirteenth century that families with several houses would take their windows round with them on their travels.

ABOVE The south tower and great hall built by Laurence de Ludlow in the last years of the thirteenth century. The outside stairway provides access to the solar and, via a drawbridge, to the tower.

LEFT The exterior of the great hall and the north tower, with its half-timbered domestic quarters.

Laurence provided himself with that rarest and most precious of medieval domestic commodities – privacy – by building a solar adjoining the hall on the south side. It can only be reached by going outside from the hall and climbing an external stairway; thus privacy and protection were afforded simultaneously. The family, however, had ample opportunity to see what was going on in the hall beneath, as we can see from the two splendid 'squints' flanking the fireplace.

To the north tower Laurence added a delightfully timbered projecting upper storey to give his family even greater privacy. The room on the second floor has a splendid medieval fireplace. It would have been to the south tower, however, that the family would have retired in case of danger, for the only direct access to it was from the solar, by a drawbridge from a platform outside the entrance. The walls of this tower are 1·5 metres (5 feet) thick, and a staircase rises in three stages from the ground floor to the roof within the thickness of the wall on the courtyard side – the side which would have been furthest from any fighting. The walls contain garderobes or privies which discharged into the moat below – further evidence of medieval 'home comforts' – and the tower is surmounted by an observation turret commanding a fine view of the Onny Valley.

Time, decay and accident (such as the early nineteenth-century fire which broke out in the south tower when it was a blacksmith's shop) have left their marks. But careful and scholarly care have ensured that Stokesay Castle, with its neighbouring church, gives the visitor a unique opportunity to sense the flavour of manorial life in the years when, however well a rich man might provide himself with creature comforts, he dare not neglect to surround them with adequate defences.

# 5 TUDORS AND

ITH THE DEATH OF RICHARD III in 1485 on the battlefield of Bosworth, a generation of civil strife came to an end. The age of the Tudors had begun, and although in 1511, in the second year 'of the reyne of Kynge Henri the VIII', the Duke of Buckingham emblazoned his arms and titles above the gateway of his fine new 'castle' at Thornbury in Gloucestershire, real castle building in England and Wales was at an end. Thornbury might have looked like a medieval castle but it was in fact one of the first great country houses foreshadowed by those increasingly comfortable fortified manor houses of the later Middle Ages.

Henry VIII's reign witnessed a major social revolution. The enormous estates of the medieval church were confiscated, their great abbeys and monasteries closed. The new generation who acquired their wealth from the king were themselves founding powerful dynasties. Often using the monastic buildings as quarries, they erected vast and imposing – and totally unfortified – residences to proclaim their arrival in the establishment and their position in it. The penalty for forfeiting the royal favour could be high (Thornbury's Duke of Buckingham lost both his head and his castle) but the prize for 'keeping in' was great and there was little domestic turbulence to fear, a happy fact that was reflected in the acres of glass that the new families such as the Cavendishes, the Thynnes and the Cecils incorporated in their palatial homes. Not that the reigns of Henry VIII and his children were without moments of crisis. In Henry's own reign, for instance, there was the rising known as the 'Pilgrimage of Grace' in the north of the country, and on his son's death in 1554 there was an attempt by the Duke of Northumberland to put a young queen, Lady Jane Grey, on the throne in the place of the rightful successor, Mary Tudor. At times like this the old castles again came into use. Queen Mary gathered her forces at Framlingham in Suffolk, ready to assert her authority over the rebellion. And in the border country of the north, and along the Welsh Marches, castles continued to play an important defensive and administrative role. The Royal Council of the North was based on York Castle and the Council of the Marches at Ludlow.

In the north in 1569, when there was a rising against Elizabeth by those who supported Mary Queen of Scots, a number of castles, including Durham and Newcastle, played a part. Castles made useful prisons too. Mary Queen of Scots herself spent almost two decades in captivity : among the castles she stayed at were Carlisle in Cumbria, Bolton in Lancashire, Tutbury in Staffordshire and Fotheringhay in Northamptonshire, where she was finally executed because Elizabeth and her advisers thought it too dangerous to have her living as a rallying point while the threat of a Spanish invasion loomed large.

However, some advanced and important new fortifications were built by the Tudors. These were the coastal castles built to repel foreign invaders. We have seen how Edward III built a fortress at Queenborough to guard one of the most vital approaches to the Thames when there was a grave threat of a French invasion. The next real invasion scare came in the wake of Henry VIII's breach with Rome,

# STUARTS

ABOVE LEFT Walmer, official residence of the Lords Warden of the Cinque Ports.

ABOVE RIGHT Cannons point through the embrasures of St Mawe's castle to sweep the waters of Carrick Roads. The ports are splayed to provide the maximum field of fire.

with the attempts of the Pope to marshall the forces of the Catholic powers against the king he had excommunicated. So during the two years between 1538 and 1540 Henry, in a typically vigorous response, erected the most comprehensive system of coastal defences since the Romans had set England's coastline under the Count of the Saxon Shore. In all he built a chain of more than twenty coastal forts and blockhouses from Hull on the north-east coast to Milford Haven in Wales – and this was in addition to existing castles, such as Dover in Kent and Carisbrooke on the Isle of Wight, which he strengthened and extended.

Henry's most famous castles were Sandown in Sussex, and Deal and Walmer in Kent, ('three new blockhouses to be made in the Downs') and Southsea, guarding Portsmouth Harbour, which he designed himself. These were artillery forts rather than traditional castles. They were of 'clover leaf' pattern, designed to function with the smallest possible garrison and the heaviest possible fortification. They generally had a central tower protected by a cluster of outer bastions, and they lay sunk into the ground so as not to present too conspicuous a target. Their main cannons had a range of up to 2·2 kilometres ($1\frac{1}{2}$ miles), and their moats were entirely covered from gun ports in their outer bastions.

Henry had two thousand men at a time working on his Downs castles alone and, like Edward III before him, relied upon press gangs to recruit his labour. Most of the stone came from nearby monasteries. His finest castle was Deal, which we will come to later, but Walmer is still used as the official residence of the Lords Warden of the Cinque Ports. The Duke of Wellington, who reckoned it the finest coastal residence in the kingdom, died here.

Henry called extensively upon the services of Continental military engineers and architects both for his southern and his northern castles, for he had to guard against danger from the 'auld alliance' of France and Scotland, which was especially close at this time. He built Lindisfarne castle on Holy Island and transformed Carlisle from a medieval castle into a major border fortress with a garrison of eight hundred mercenaries.

Invasion threats persisted right through the first thirty years of the reign of Elizabeth (1558–1603). She was not a great castle builder though, preferring to improve and adapt what she inherited. Like her father she used the services of foreign experts. An Italian called Gianibelli was her favourite and he was employed at Carisbrooke, and at Tilbury at the mouth of the Thames, where Elizabeth virtually rebuilt one of her father's early forts. It was here, in the year of the Armada (1588), that she made the most famous speech of her life to her assembled troops.

Elizabeth's most important work, however, was at Berwick in Northumberland, where we can still see much of the imposing curtain wall, with its huge regularly spaced bastions heavily mounted with guns to rake the ditch below.

Few of Henry Tudor's fortresses saw any action. The Scots and the French did not invade, and when the Armada came 'the winds blew and they were scattered'. But within forty years of Elizabeth's death England was once more torn by civil war. During the struggle between king and Parliament, castles again came into their own. From that day in August 1642 when Charles raised his standard at Nottingham until Raglan fell after a ten week siege four years later, castles played a crucial part in the war. It was not just great medieval castles that were pressed into service. So were town walls and many of the fortified manor houses of the later Middle Ages. That they proved their worth was testified by the fact that so many were slighted when they were eventually taken.

At the beginning of the war most of the castles were in Royalist hands, and their owners brought over experts from the Continent, especially from the Low Countries (where they had recent experience of civil war), to strengthen them. Portsmouth in Hampshire, Hull in Yorkshire, Oxford, the king's capital, and Newark in Nottinghamshire were just four of the towns that were given additional defences – ramparts and bastions outside the walls,

Cannons in action in a sixteenth-century Portuguese battle scene. Barrels came in a range of sizes, but the very largest of them were occasionally dummies, used in a sort of early psychological warfare, with the real, much smaller barrels lashed on top.

Camber, a low-lying blockhouse on the Downs built by Henry VIII as part of his string of coastal defences.

with detached works still further outside to draw fire and hold up the advance of the enemy. It was a costly business. At Barnstaple in Devon the Parliamentarians spent £1,120 on materials and wages alone and another £450 in 'entrenching the town' and 'in fortifying the castle, building three defensible gates and making sixteen platforms, £660.' Ditches were reinforced by wooden palisades to provide an effective deterrent against cavalry charges.

Charles's capital for much of the Civil War was Oxford, and this became the best defended city in the kingdom. All male inhabitants of the place were pressed into service to raise fortifications, and £30,000 was spent. The city remained in the king's hands until the war was lost, but unlike the other great stronghold at Newark it did not have to withstand great siege or bombardment. It took the Parliamentary forces three sieges and nearly four years to subdue Newark. Surrender came only when the garrison had been reduced to eating their own horses and the plague had broken out.

The two castles which held out the longest and whose fall marked the final eclipse of the king's chances were Pendennis in Cornwall and Raglan. There was even a brief revival of interest in castles after their surrender, for during the so-called second Civil War from 1646 to 1648 a number of Welsh castles – such as Tenby, Chirk, Chepstow and Pembroke – went over to the king. It was Cromwell's annoyance at such resistance that led him to insist on slighting castles wherever possible.

With the execution of the king in 1649 the age of the English castle finally came to an end, but in the aftermath of the Restoration came peace and plenty and a gradual reawakening of interest in, and affection for, the castle as a symbol of something romantic and chivalrous and well worth recreating.

# DEAL CASTLE

## KENT

OWHERE in Europe is there anything quite like the system of coastal fortifications built by Henry VIII during the few years after 1538 when, the Pope having arranged a truce between the king of France and the great Habsburg ruler Charles V, England faced the prospect of invasion from a briefly united Catholic Europe determined to bring her back into the fold.

Not since the Count of the Saxon Shore had sought to provide a comprehensive network of coastal defences had Europe's only island power been so carefully guarded against aggression from the Continental mainland. Of course these were not true castles in the medieval sense. They were not meant to be residences but were exclusively military buildings erected by the king as national defences. They ringed the coast from Hull to Milford Haven. There were a cluster of five on the Thames at Tilbury and Gravesend. There were three at Dover and others on the Isle of Wight and in Cornwall. Southsea Castle, built to guard Portsmouth Harbour, was designed by the king himself, and it is possible that he had a hand in the most important forts of all – the three castles which 'keep the Downs'. These, 'the King's new block houses or Bulwarks', were, from north to south, Sandown, Deal and Walmer. Of these the largest and by far the most impressive and authentic now is Deal. Of Sandown little remains. Walmer was transformed into what the Duke of Wellington described as 'the most charming of marine residences'. The queen, he alleged, had nothing to compare with it. Deal was turned into a residence at one stage but nothing remains of those domestic additions, and what we have now,

OPPOSITE An aerial view of Deal, the most sophisticated of Henry's artillery forts, looking much as it did in his day. The remarkable clover leaf pattern provided three tiers of platforms for long-range cannon and as many as 145 handgun embrasures.

apart from the battlements which date from the mid-eighteenth century, is a coastal fort almost exactly as Henry VIII built it.

The Downs castles were built very quickly indeed. The three stout bastions, linked by earth bulwarks into one defensive system, were completed within eighteen months, by the

Henry VIII, the greatest royal fortress builder of post-medieval times.

autumn of 1540. The stone used was mainly Caen, quarried from the dissolved Carmelite Priory at Sandwich and other south coast monastic buildings. Pressed labour was used and at one stage during the summer of 1539 some 2,000 men were employed on Deal alone. They were none too pleased with the 5d a day the king gave them, and a threat to withhold their labour pending the payment of 6d led to nine of their ringleaders being promptly jailed.

Deal was built to be manned by the astonishingly small garrison of a captain and twenty-four men. It was certainly the best fortified of Henry's coastal forts and indeed is among the most strongly fortified of any castle built anywhere at any time. It was built on a double clover leaf design with two rings of six semicircular bastions surrounding a round central tower. An impressive array of long-

range cannons was mounted on this tower and on the encircling bastions. Those facing the seaward side could rake the whole of the Downs anchorage and act as a powerful deterrent to any invading force. Should such a force have landed they would have found the castle's defences formidable. The entrance was protected by a drawbridge and portcullis with five vertical murder holes in the roof of the passageway above, through which defenders could have bombarded any assailing force sent to breach the massive iron-studded oak door – which still survives. Placed between the outer curtain wall and the keep is, in effect, a high-level inner moat. This was commanded by gun ports or musket embrasures on the ground floor of the bastions, just as the moat proper is commanded by gun ports in the outer curtain and its bastion. In all there were five tiers of gun ports and at least 145 openings for firearms. Although many of these became windows in the eighteenth and nineteenth centuries, a number of the original openings still survive to give an indication of how formidable any attacker would have found the castle.

Its armoury doubtless included sakers, which used 2·7-kilo (6-pound) shot, culverins of 3·6 kilos (8 pounds), basilisks of 11·3 kilos (25 pounds) and demi-cannon of 14·5 kilos (32 pounds) – an intimidating arsenal. There was a furnace for heating round shot and plenty of storage space where large quantities of powder could be kept secure and dry. There were stores for food and drink in the basement, and on the ground floor a kitchen, a bakery and accommodation for the soldiers, all planned to ensure that the fortress could withstand a siege. On the first floor there were more comfortable quarters for the captain and other senior members of the garrison. All the rooms were grouped round a central tower, which was in effect a hollow pillar, with the castle well in the basement. The accommodation was improved in the seventeenth and eighteenth centuries, and other comforts and a chapel were incorporated. It is, therefore, impossible to be precise about the use to which all the apartments were originally put, although in recent times certain clues such as fireplaces and other original features have been discovered behind later panelling.

It was a measure of its formidable success as a deterrent that Deal Castle was never attacked or besieged by those against whom Henry armed himself. It remained garrisoned as a coastal fortress, however, throughout the rest of the century and was well prepared to withstand the Spaniards at the time of the Armada in 1588. It was then neglected and fell into some disrepair until 1634, when it was

BELOW The passage leading to the basement under the keep. At the far end is the well which served the garrison.

surveyed by the King's Engineer for Fortifications who estimated the repair bill at £1,243. 16s.

The castle fell into the hands of the Parliamentarians at the beginning of the Civil War but without any fighting. However, in 1648, troops in Kent rebelled for the king and Deal surrendered. It then saw action for the first and only time in its history. Together with Walmer and Sandown it was besieged by the Parliamentarians. The Royalist fleet suffered many casualties in trying to relieve it, and on 14 August 1648 Colonel Rich, the Parliamentary Commander, reported to the Speaker of the House of Commons a great victory against eight hundred Royalists, with eighty of the enemy killed and a hundred taken prisoner, and only seven casualties on the Parliamentary side. On 25 August the castle was captured.

It was prepared for action again when the Dutch sailed up the Thames in the time of Charles II, and there was a flurry of excitement at the 'bloodless' revolution of 1688 when it was thought the castle might feature in an engagement between William III and James II.

In the eighteenth century the cap-

tain of Deal Castle was one of the principal lieutenants of the Lord Warden of the Cinque Ports, and it was, for a time, like Walmer, transformed into a residence. Most of the domestic additions were destroyed by a German bomb in the Second World War and because of this it was decided to restore the castle, as nearly as possible, to its original condition. So today we can see Deal almost as Henry VIII envisaged it. In two of the rooms are displays of photographs and prints illustrating his defensive system. The rest of the castle is now given over to a museum devoted to the archaeology of Deal and the surrounding district.

ABOVE The outer bastions on which the main armament was mounted. The guns here today are 32-pounders of George IV's reign. Both the moat and the courtyard, which runs between the outer and inner bastions, could be covered by small-arms fire from gunports near water level.

# PENDENNIS CASTLE

## CORNWALL

In 1595, seven years after the Spanish Armada had been scattered by the winds and chased by Elizabeth's admirals, four Spanish galleons descended on the Cornish coast and sacked Penzance, Mousehole and Newlyn. Two years later the Spaniards attempted to invade Falmouth, and with talk of another Armada a decade after the first, the privy council decided that the coastal defences in these parts should be strengthened. So it was that four hundred men were set to work at Pendennis at the beginning of 1598. For the next eighteen months they laboured to surround Henry VIII's fort with the 1·6-hectare (4-acre), star-shaped enclosure which made this so impregnable a fortress that fifty years later it was the last castle on English soil to surrender during the Civil War.

Pendennis, and the neighbouring castle of St Mawes across Falmouth Bay, which between them guarded the entrance to Carrick Roads, were among the last of Henry VIII's great coastal defences built against that earlier threat of invasion in 1540. Pendennis itself was not completed until about 1545, a sturdy blockhouse on a promontory, with a much smaller one, Little Dennis, on the rocks below. This had been reckoned a strategic site before the Romans came; there had almost certainly been a major Iron Age hillfort here.

Henry's fort, under its governor John Killigrew, saw no action, and it must have been somewhat neglected after the threat of invasion had subsided for the privy council to decide that it needed such improvement fifty years later.

Thereafter, though no second Armada materialized and there were no further threats from France or Spain, Pendennis was obviously kept in good repair. In the Civil War it was early recognized as one of the king's crucial strongholds and heavily gar-

risoned. Henrietta Maria came here briefly *en route* for France in 1644, after the birth of her daughter at Exeter, and Charles, Prince of Wales, was here too in February and early March of 1646, just before the castle began the five most dramatic months in its history.

The Civil War was nearing its end. Only in a few outposts did the Royalist cause burn bright. Even Oxford, royal capital for most of the war, was on the verge of capitulation when in March 1646 Fairfax, commander of Cromwell's army, advanced into Cornwall. St Mawes surrendered on the 12th without a struggle, and on the 18th the Parliamentary forces arrived at Pendennis and the garrison was called upon to surrender.

The call provoked a firm and ringing refusal from the commander of the garrison. Colonel John Arundell from Trerice, near Newlyn, was one of the king's most loyal subjects. He was known affectionately as 'Jack for the King' or 'Old Tilbury' because he had been present at Tilbury in 1588 when Queen Elizabeth had made her famous address to her troops on the eve of the Armada. He had sat in Parliament for St Mawes in 1624 and 1628, and in 1643, when he was about seventy, he was appointed Governor of Pendennis.

Asked to surrender he replied, 'I will here bury myself before I deliver up this castle to such as fight against His Majesty'. For some months this seemed precisely what he would do. In April he curtly rejected another summons to surrender, and this in spite of the fact that the castle was besieged

OPPOSITE Pendennis, as it appeared when besieged by the Parliamentarians in 1646, showing Henry VIII's fortress in its Elizabethan enclosure, and the smaller blockhouse of Little Dennis guarding the south-eastern tip of the promontory. The castle is ideally sited on a steep-sided flat-topped headland surrounded on three sides by the sea, and its design is so efficient that it survived longer in Royalist hands than any other English castle.

The Civil War protagonists – Charles I and his Parliamentarian adversary Oliver Cromwell.

on the landward side and blockaded from the sea. No supplies could get through, even though there were attempts to bring them over from St Malo on the Brittany coast. By the end of July things were getting desperate. On the 26th Arundell sent a message to Prince Charles saying they could not hold out much longer without relief. He sent men from the garrison to try and bring supplies in, but their boats were bombarded and many of them were killed or wounded.

No relief came, and at last on 17 August Pendennis, the last English castle in Royalist hands, surrendered, just two days before Raglan, in Wales, also fell. Arundell and his garrison were granted full military honours and twenty-four officers and nine hundred men were allowed to march out, 'flying colours, trumpets sounding, drums beating, matches lighted at both ends, bullets in their mouths, and every soldier twelve charges of powder'. It was a proud garrison but a battered one; many of them succumbed fairly quickly to the privations of the siege which they had endured with such fortitude.

It was the last time Pendennis was to play any significant part in England's history. The castle was

garrisoned throughout the eighteenth century, and indeed had a governor as late as 1837. In the Napoleonic Wars French prisoners were kept here and it formed part of Britain's official coastal defences in the First World War. After that it was scheduled as an ancient monument and given into the care of the state, only to be brought back into service and repossessed by the army during the Second World War. Since 1946, however, it has been a much visited monument again.

Pendennis is really two fortresses. Firstly there is the central blockhouse within the Elizabethan enclosure, consisting of a keep with a curtain wall around it. The keep itself is divided into two: a central tower three storeys high and a two-storey rectangular tower which housed the domestic quarters of the governor. The curtain wall is strongly defended. The principal entrance to the keep is by a drawbridge over a dry ditch, and the entrance is further guarded by a massive portcullis. The gun ports are splayed so as to allow the widest range of fire, and here would have been stationed the culverins, cannon and demi-cannon with which the bay and the entrance to Carrick Roads could have been raked. All of the main castle

ABOVE From a gunport at Pendennis the castle of St Mawes can be seen on the far side of Falmouth Bay. These two fortresses were built within a year of each other by Henry VIII, to guard against invasion in 1540.

ABOVE Little Dennis, crouched on a rock beneath the main blockhouse. It has been in ruins since the Civil War.

LEFT The curtain wall and the two-part keep. The governor was housed in the rectangular block to the left. In the foreground are gun emplacements of the Second World War.

is in a remarkably good state of preservation, but Little Dennis has been in ruins since soon after the siege.

The second and enclosing fort, covering some 1·6 hectares (4 acres), consists of walls with embrasures for cannons and a steep stone revetted ditch around the whole of the head-land. There is little wonder that this took eighteen months to complete. Even the defences were not entirely finished. The outer gateway was not completed until 1611. Henry's fort was little altered then or later, but the outer defences were further strengthened and improved in both the eighteenth and nineteenth centuries.

As at Deal, there is an exhibition here describing Henry VIII's system of coastal defences, but it takes little knowledge or imagination to understand why this fortress, further improved by the greatest of the Tudor monarchs, was such a formidable stronghold. Only starvation brought about by a long siege could have forced any defender to yield. Today we can look out from the turret over Falmouth to St Mawes or the sea and share some of the secure confidence that 'Old Tilbury' must have felt when he made his defiant rejoinder to the first demands for his sword.

# RAGLAN CASTLE

## GWENT

'THE FIRST fortified and last 'rendered' castle in the Civil War, Raglan was also the last medieval castle to be built on the truly grand scale. Its massive fortifications are as impressive and its brief history as fascinating as that of any castle in Britain.

There were few, if any, traces of the Norman motte-and-bailey castle when Sir William ap Thomas, the Blue Knight of Gwent, chose this site for his fortress in the Welsh Marches around 1430. Sir William, Steward of the Lordship of Usk and Caerleon, trusty servant of Richard, Duke of York, and an early champion of the Yorkist cause, was anxious to safeguard his territorial position in the south-eastern March. His violent assertion of his own influence, as when he used a band of eighty armed men to enforce the appointment of a local prior, is typical of the rough manner in which authority was wielded and territory controlled in these parts at that time. It illustrated why Sir William himself felt that a strong base was essential to maintaining his position.

Sir William died in 1445 and the castle was completed by his son, Sir William Herbert. Like his father, he was a staunch Yorkist, and when Edward of York won the battle of Mortimer's Cross in 1461 and came to the throne as Edward IV his career prospered greatly. He was made Earl of Pembroke, Chief Justice and Chamberlain of South Wales, a Knight of the Garter, and later Chief Justice of North Wales as well. Unfortunately fortunes ebbed and flowed during the Wars of the Roses, and in 1469 he was defeated at Edgecot near Northampton and beheaded. But by then the castle at

Raglan was complete and a fitting expression of the power he had enjoyed.

In the sixteenth century the residential quarters were improved and extended, and by the beginning of the seventeenth century Raglan was as strong a castle and as splendid a residence as any in the kingdom. By

An aerial view of Raglan, as formidable and splendid as any castle in the kingdom. Behind the gatehouse is the Pitched Stone Court, and to the left the grassed Fountain Court, originally surrounded by palatial domestic apartments. Linking the two are the buttery and great hall. Steps lead down beside the foundations of the chapel, above which ran the gallery.

this time the Herberts, who had enjoyed high favour at the court of Elizabeth and maintained their influence under James I, were laden with honours and titles, the most important of which was the Earldom of Worcester.

It was the sixth earl, later marquess, of Worcester who, at the outbreak of the Civil War in 1642, garrisoned Raglan for the king. A man of considerable learning and scientific knowledge, who installed hydraulic machinery in the castle and amassed a wonderful library and a great collection of rare treasures, the marquess was first and foremost the loyalest of loyal subjects. Reputed to be the richest man in the kingdom, it was said that he spent a million pounds on the Royalist cause and some £40,000 on keeping the garrison at Raglan alone. He entrusted the defence of the castle to his younger son, Lord Charles Somerset, who, to repel the enemy, built a great battery, 457 metres (500 yards) north-east of the gatehouse, and created a new outwork covering the south-east and north sides of the castle, where attackers were most likely to approach. This formidable fortress was not besieged until 1646, by which time the king's cause was lost. 'Raglan and Pendennis', we are told, 'like winter fruit, hung long on'.

When action came it was vigorous. Fairfax besieged the castle, which had a garrison of some eight hundred men, with 1,500 troops, swollen to 3,500 after the fall of Oxford. Daily the Great Tower was bombarded with 9-kilo (20-pound) shot and with mortar shells. So strong was the tower that little damage was done, although the mortar caused considerable casual-

ties. For almost three months the garrison held out, finally surrendering, only because there was no hope of relief, two days after the fall of Pendennis on 19 August 1646.

The garrison was allowed to leave, with drums beating and colours flying, the officers retaining their arms. The castle itself was less generously treated. It was plundered of its contents, its wonderful library burned, its fortifications slighted and the Great Tower itself mined – just as Rochester had been mined 400 years before. The fall of Raglan, which Parliament celebrated with a service of thanksgiving, marked the end of the first Civil War, and the end of the castle's active life.

Though the Somerset family prospered after the Restoration and became Dukes of Beaufort, the family seat was shifted to Badminton in Gloucestershire, and Raglan, although it remained in their possession, was left a ruin. Used as a quarry in the eighteenth century, in the nineteenth there were suggestions that it should be reconstructed to 'combine ancient magnificence with modern accommodation' – but nothing came of the scheme. The ruins were safeguarded, however, and were among the most popular romantic ruins of the age. Finally, just before the Second World War they were given into the care of the state by the Duke of Beaufort.

Enough remains for us to appreciate the strength and understand the design of the castle. The most notable feature of Raglan is the Great Tower, the Yellow Tower of Gwent. This was built by Sir William ap Thomas between 1435 and his death ten years later. It is a great hexagonal tower with walls 3 metres (10 feet) thick, and is in effect a fortress in its own right for it is surrounded entirely by water and approached only across a drawbridge from the rest of the castle buildings. As at Bodiam, the owner had regard to the potential unreliability of his retainers. Raglan's strength was tested in the Civil War bombardment, when though the

battlements were damaged the main structure survived intact.

Sir William also supervised the building of the south gate, but almost all of the rest of the castle was the work of his son. This main enclosure is arranged round two courts, with the main residential buildings, themselves improved in Elizabethan times, lying between them. The Fountain Court was surrounded by the principal

LEFT The gatehouse and, in the foreground, the great Yellow Tower of Gwent, one of the finest towers built in England during the fifteenth century. A symbol of feudalism, it was mined shortly after Raglan surrendered in 1646, and the fall of this last Royalist stronghold marked the end of the first Civil War.

BELOW The residential buildings around the Fountain Court, showing the grand staircase to the apartments in the upper storey. The square of stone marks the site of 'a pleasant marble fountain in the midst thereof called the White Horse, continually running with a clear water'.

apartments and the Pitched Stone Court to the north was devoted to the service quarters. There are a number of hexagonal towers around the whole enclosure, most of them with gun ports. There were gun ports too in the Great Gate, which was originally defended by a drawbridge, two portcullises and three double doors as well. There was of course added protection for both the main gate and the south gate from the Great Tower itself.

Before its destruction, Raglan, with its courtyards, noble hall, long gallery, libraries, and the many treasures it contained, the whole guarded by a tower surpassing, we are told, 'for height, strength and neatness ... most, if not every other tower in England and Wales', was indeed a fitting seat for the richest man in the land. Today its ruins are sufficient to remind us that even in an age when powerful cannons had replaced stone-throwing siege engines a great castle in the medieval style could still be a formidable stronghold.

The gatehouse and entrance archway, seen from the Pitched Stone Court. On the left is the Closet Tower.

# 6 SCOTTISH

THE CASTLES OF SCOTLAND deserve a sumptuous volume of their own. All we can do here is whet the appetite by taking three representative examples from the wealth of Scottish castles, many still occupied by the families who built them and adapted them over the centuries. There is no accurate count of the number of fortified houses and castles in Scotland but there are well over a thousand dating from the seventeenth century or before. Not only are the Scottish castles a rich and varied heritage but they were more regularly used for military purposes than their

The beautiful thirteenth-century sandstone castle of Caerlaverock, famous for its siege in 1300 and unusual for its triangular plan. This view shows the south side, with Murdoch's Tower in the foreground and the twin-towered gatehouse to the left.

# CASTLES

Built in 1394 on the site of a Pictish promontory fort, Dunnottar is almost unassailable. It can be approached on the landward side only by a narrow path that drops nearly to the sea before climbing to the gatehouse and the L-shaped tower-house keep.

Linlithgow, a medieval castle transformed into a Scottish Renaissance palace. It was the birthplace of James v of Scotland and of his daughter, Mary Queen of Scots, and the favourite residence of many Scottish kings. Charles I also stayed here, and the castle was refortified by Cromwell. It was finally destroyed by fire after the Jacobite Rebellion in 1745.

English counterparts. Long after crenellation had become little more than a decoration in England, fortification was essential north of the border. Castles played a part in the Jacobite Risings of 1715 and 1745 (when Edinburgh was taken and its castle remained in Hanoverian hands). And it was in the little remembered Rising of 1719 that Eilean Donan, the last British castle to be smashed into submission, was bombarded by English warships.

The Scottish castles fall into three broad groups : the great strongholds built by Scotland's kings or premier nobles ; the multitude of fortified tower houses, many of which are still lived in ; and an impressive collection of Scottish baronial castles of the late eighteenth and the nineteenth centuries.

Of the earliest Scottish castles we have few traces and little knowledge, for they were works of earth and wood. There was very little in the way of stone building before the mid-thirteenth century. By then, however, Scotland's kings and contesting barons had almost caught up with military architecture south of the border, and during the next three centuries built a succession of remarkable fortresses from which the most unmanageable country north of the Alps was controlled. Of these, the two most important strategically were at Edinburgh, where the Scottish capital was dominated by a castle rising sheer from the rocks above the city, and Stirling, the gateway to the Highlands, if anything an even more imposing sight. Other great Scottish castles that are especially worthy of note are Castle Urquhart, on a promontory in Loch Ness, Dunnottar, off the coast of Grampian, and Tantallon, Lothian, the home of Black Douglas. Some of the castles are as graceful as they are strong. Linlithgow Palace, also in Lothian and now an empty ruin, was a favourite residence of many Scottish kings, and at Blair Atholl, Tayside, the Dukes of Atholl (who still muster from their retainers the only remaining private army in the United Kingdom) created a stately home from their rugged fortress. Blair was the last mainland castle to withstand a siege – in 1746. Culzean, in Strathclyde, was graciously transformed by Robert Adam in the 1780s. The romantic Dunvegan on Skye, with its associations with the Pretender and with Dr Johnson and Walter Scott, also became a comfortable country house.

There are particularly imposing castles in the border counties, of which the most spectacular is

a) A cutaway section through a spacious and luxurious L-shaped tower house. The storerooms, great hall, with window recess, and principal bedchamber are in the main block to the right, while the taller wing houses the small private rooms.

b) At this more modest tower house, attackers are trying to break in by ramming the heavy, studded door of the ground floor cattle-byre and by setting fire to the building with flaming torches. In the main hall defenders hastily pull up the ladder leading from the ground to the main entrance on the first floor, and, above, a man climbs up through a trap door to join two others who are already hurling missiles from the battlements on to the attackers below.

probably Caerlaverock in Dumfries and Galloway. Today a romantic and evocative ruin, one can well imagine the five sieges it endured; nonetheless, it has within its courtyard a set of splendid Renaissance-style apartments. Another great fortress in this region, and a grimmer one, is the Hermitage, in the Borders. It was restored in the 1820s with remarkable fidelity, and today looks much as it must have done when the Douglas family occupied it in the fifteenth century.

The second group of Scottish castles are the tower houses. The pele towers of the border country echo their southern neighbours. Those most typically Scottish are generally further north: Crathes, Craigievar and Castle Fraser in Grampian, Crichton in Lothian, Glamis in Tayside, and Threave in Dumfries and Galloway. Many of these, like the great strongholds, have been adapted and adopted for more comfortable domestic use over the centuries.

Some of the fortresses and some of the tower houses have been so much altered that they fall into the category of 'new' castles. Dunrobin in the Highlands is one of these. Here, in the middle of the last century, the Duke of Sutherland totally transformed his small medieval castle into a spectacular example of the Scottish baronial style, an example perhaps only surpassed by Victoria and Albert who gave a great face-lift to 'the pretty little castle in the old Scotch style' which they bought unseen at Balmoral.

# CRATHES CASTLE

## GRAMPIAN

ARCHITECTURE expresses both the needs and the aspirations of its age. As the need for security was first matched and then exceeded by the desire for comfort, the castle was replaced in England by the country house. In Scotland where there was, for much longer, a need for protection against marauding bands, the castle generally evolved into the tower house. The tower house was the uniquely Scottish architectural expression of the status and independence of its owner, and it helped to inspire the style that we know as Scottish baronial, which exercised a predominating influence over Scottish domestic architecture on the grand scale well into the nineteenth century.

Crathes is one of the supreme examples of the sixteenth-century tower house. It is a remarkable witness to the mason's skill in containing all the requirements for sophisticated living within the constraints of a form that was still outwardly defensive, and where grace and grandeur were combined to a remarkable degree. It was not only the need for careful comfort which inspired the development of the tower house, but natural circumstances too. In Scotland there was an acute scarcity of timber fit for building. As late as the eighteenth century Dr Johnson remarked on the lack of trees in the Scottish landscape. Such native pine and oak as there was was therefore in great demand, and importing was a costly and hazardous enterprise. To build upwards rather than outwards was consequently a manifestation of Scottish carefulness with scarce resources. At Crathes the whole roof area covers a mere 548 square metres (1,800 square feet) and the entire first floor and most of the

ABOVE Crathes' elegantly tapering tower, crowned with chimneys and projecting corner turrets.

second is carried on stone vaulting.

Although the shortage of timber encouraged the development of tall and slender buildings, the evolution of the tower house from the medieval castle was marked in other ways also evident at Crathes. The native granite was superbly strong but the most difficult stone to carve. So it was elegantly rounded, in keeping with a long tradition based on the knowledge that enemies found it easier to prise the stones from, and thus weaken, an angular building. The turrets too hark back to a more military architecture, when conically roofed, sentrybox-like structures afforded some protection at the end of the ramparts to those charged with defending the castle.

Thus the shortage of one material, the use of the most typically Scottish of building stones, and the transition to increased domesticity against a

background of civil turbulence, all find expression in this particularly beautiful Scottish tower house.

Crathes was probably longer in the building than any other house in Scotland in the sixteenth century. It was begun by Alexander Burnett, descendant of a family that had played a distinguished but not too conspicuous part in Scottish history since the days of King David in the twelfth century. The family was of Anglo-Saxon origin, and Alexander's ancestors had given loyal service to Robert the Bruce and been rewarded with extensive estates. Tradition has it that that grant of land was symbolized by the token of a beautiful hunting horn, and to this day the Horn of Leys, the history of which is not documented but which almost certainly dates from the fourteenth century, hangs in a glass case in the high hall at Crathes.

Alexander began building in 1553, but Crathes was not habitable until forty years later. Following the death of Alexander and his son and grandson in the space of a few years, his great-grandson, another Alexander, moved in and supervised the completion of the building and its internal decoration. The castle that we see is not entirely as Alexander left it. A hundred years later, at the beginning of the eighteenth century, his great-great-grandson built on a wing, known as the Queen Anne wing, partly to make the castle more fashionably elegant and partly to house his twenty-one children. In the process he

OPPOSITE Crathes, home of the Burnetts for 400 years, towers above its clipped yew hedges. To the right is the wing rebuilt after the fire of 1966.

removed the surrounding defensive wall, or barmkin, a feature of most tower houses, and laid out the garden which is such an attractive feature of Crathes today. The Queen Anne wing itself was destroyed in a fire in 1966 and has been replaced by a lower

The high hall, where the lairds of Crathes often sat in judgement in the Baron's Court. Over the fireplace hangs the castle's most prized possession, the ivory hunting horn known as the Horn of Leys, said to have been given to Robert Burnett by Robert the Bruce in 1323 to symbolize the grant of the lands of Crathes. In return for the land, Burnett was required to administer the Royal Forest of Drum, and the horn was intended as a badge of office.

structure more in keeping architecturally with the original Crathes.

The massive granite walls of the castle taper slightly towards the top, and this feature, together with the simplicity of the lower storeys, makes the structure especially elegant. It has a splendidly varied skyline of turrets, gables and corbels, but the real joy of the castle is inside, in its beautiful painted ceilings. There is really nothing at all like them in England though such ceilings are not at all uncommon in France and Germany, and there are several examples in Scotland, which looked more to the Continent than to England for inspiration in the sixteenth century. The Crathes ceilings, however, are especially fine and remarkably complete, partly because

their painted beams were boxed in with a covering of lathe and plaster by the third baronet at the end of the seventeenth century and not revealed again, in all their pristine glory, until 1877. They are evocative of the learning and interests of the cultivated sixteenth-century gentleman whose interests spanned the arts, the sciences, philosophy, the classics, and morality as expressed in allegory. The Nine Worthies (Hector, Alexander, Julius Caesar, Joshua, David, Judas Maccabeus, King Arthur, Charlemagne and Godfrey de Bouillon) are depicted here and so are the Muses and the Cardinal Virtues. Most of the beams throughout the house are adorned with inscriptions, poetic, biblical and moral. Among the most interest-

ing are those in the Green Lady's room, named from the ghost that is supposed to haunt it. These include such vigorous injunctions as:

Contemne, no man in miserie,
Augment with spyt no poore man's sorrow,
For fortunes faults in constancie,
May cause his case be thine tomorrow.

It is an injunction that we can hope that the Laird of Crathes bore in mind when sitting in judgement in the Baron's Court held sometimes in the high hall downstairs or in the magnificent long gallery.

However they adjudicated on the conduct of others, the Crathes lairds certainly behaved with remarkable circumspection themselves! Sir Thomas Burnett, for instance, knighted by James I in 1620 and made one

The Muses room, with its fine William Morris tapestry, and an array of injunctions to good behaviour on its painted beams.

of the first baronets of Nova Scotia by Charles I six years later, maintained the respect of both sides in the Civil War; he thus preserved his head and his lands and saved Crathes from being requisitioned to house the soldiers of either side. In spite of a dispute over the succession in the 1760s, the Burnetts of Crathes stood aside from the turmoils of that century too and remained in possession of

the castle until General Sir James Burnett, thirteenth baronet and twenty-fifth laird, made over the castle and part of the estate to the National Trust for Scotland in 1952.

The long gallery at the top of the castle has a splendid oak-panelled ceiling – the only one of its type in Scotland.

142

# EDINBURGH CASTLE

## LOTHIAN

THE HISTORY of Scotland and the history of Edinburgh Castle are two strands, often interwoven, of the same story. Like the Tower of London, Edinburgh Castle has through the ages been both national citadel and royal palace, and much else besides. It was the home of the Treasury and of Scotland's National Records. It was a storehouse for armaments in the past and is a great armoury now. Kings have ruled from here and taken refuge here. It has been a state prison and the last bastion of lost causes. Unlike the Tower of London it has sometimes fallen, but never to open assault. It has been bombarded into surrender and starved into submission, and probably betrayed as well, but it has never been captured, save by two extraordinarily brazen surprise attacks.

No great city is more splendidly dominated by its castle. Indeed it was the position and increasing import- ance of the castle that was the most significant single factor in making Edinburgh the capital of Scotland. In the safety of the fortress James I and James II began holding regular parlia- ments in the fifteenth century and so set the seal on Edinburgh's position as the administrative centre of Scotland.

Long before then, however, the castle on the rock had become the principal home of the kings of Scotland. And long before that the strategic importance of this com- manding natural site had been recog- nized. There was a fort here in the Iron Age, and probably in the Bronze Age

The castle from the east, dominating the city from its rock and commanding the country for miles around.

too, for the rock which towers almost 92 metres (300 feet) above Princes Street – and 135 metres (443 feet) above sea level – was one of the most natural defensive positions in the British Isles, commanding the country all around, well supplied with springs of water and big enough to afford pasturage for cattle.

There are no traces of those early hillforts, nor of the fortress that the Pictish kings almost certainly had on this spot. Indeed, and here Edinburgh differs markedly from the Tower of London, there are few traces of any early medieval building, and fewer still of medieval fortifications. Bruised, battered, razed, restored:

the cycle has been repeated over the centuries, and today most of the castle dates from the sixteenth century and after. Although the buildings that are here comprise a great and secure fortress, Edinburgh Castle is more interesting for its historical associations than for its architecture.

There is but one fragment of the

EDINBURGH CASTLE
1 Esplanade
2 Dry ditch
3 Guard House
4 Inner Barrier
5 Portcullis Gate
6 The Lang Stairs
7 Mons Meg
8 St Margaret's Chapel
9 Fore Wall Battery
10 Fore Well
11 Half Moon Bastion
12 Palace or King's Lodging
13 Crown Room
14 Queen Mary's Room
15 Great Hall
16 Palace Yard or Close
17 National War Memorial
18 Foggy Gate
19 Dury's Battery
20 New Barracks
21 Governor's House
22 Hospital Buildings
23 Mill's Mount Barracks
24 Mill's Mount Battery
25 Six Gun Battery
26 The Low Defence

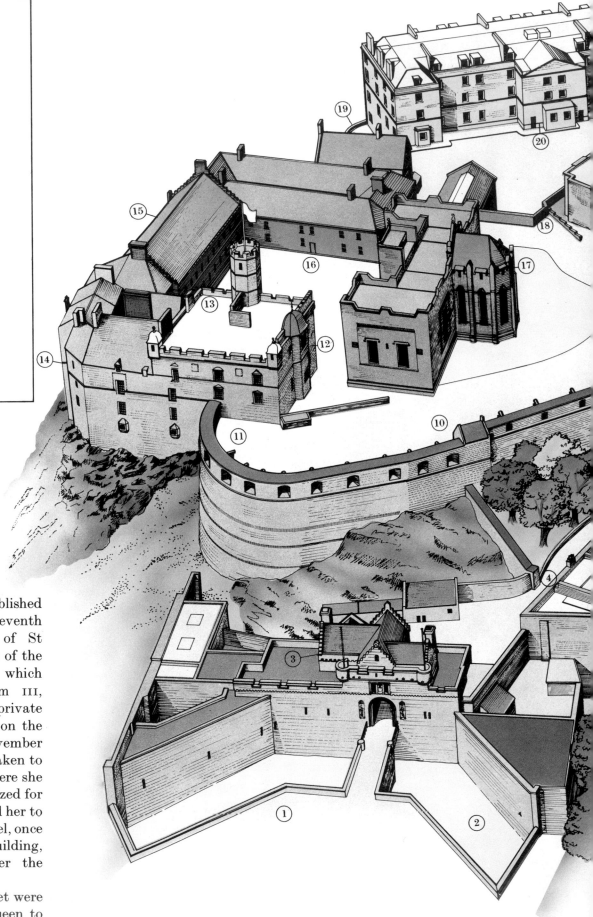

Norman castle that was established here towards the end of the eleventh century, the small chapel of St Margaret on the highest point of the rock. This is the chapel which Margaret, queen of Malcolm III, Malcolm Canmore, built for private prayer. Here she heard Mass on the day before her death on 16 November 1093, and from here she was taken to the Abbey of Dunfermline, where she still lies buried, a queen canonized for the piety of a life that endeared her to her country. But even the chapel, once a fine and simple Norman building, has been much altered over the centuries.

Malcolm and Queen Margaret were the first Scottish king and queen to live in the castle, and most medieval

kings spent much time here, summoning their councils and guarding their treasures. In 1174, however, the castle fell into English hands, for William the Lion, King of Scotland, after he had been defeated and captured at Alnwick by Henry II, was forced to deliver four Scottish castles as security for his ransom. Edinburgh was one. That was a brief English occupa-

tion, but just over a century later, in 1291, Edward I, the Hammer of the Scots, came to the castle to accept the homage of his conquered territory. Five years later he returned, bombarded the castle into submission within eight days and installed a company of 347 soldiers and attendants. His siege engines, we are told, 'cast stones over the walls, sore beating and bruising the building within'.

In 1313 English occupation ended when Sir Thomas Randolph, Earl of

Moray and nephew of Robert the Bruce, led a daring attack on the castle with a party of just thirty men, who scaled the rock on the west side, surprised the defenders and reasserted Scottish control of the fortress. Robert the Bruce then ordered the destruction of all the fortifications except St Margaret's Chapel so that Edinburgh Castle could never again be of use to the English. His designs were frustrated a few years later, however, for during the minority of King David I the English moved a garrison into the ruins and rebuilt the castle, even including stables, a tilt-yard for exercise, and gardens and orchards in their schemes.

In 1341 the tables were turned yet again, and by another surprise attack. A group of Scotsmen, disguised as merchants and led by William of Douglas, unloaded corn and wine in the entrance so that the gates could not be closed. The castle was then

ambushed and the English were ejected. It remained in Scottish hands for the next three centuries and was extended and strengthened by successive Scottish kings.

The Scottish kings did not always enjoy their associations with the castle. Several ascended the throne during their minorities and were used as pawns by warfaring factions, just as James VI of Scotland and I of England had been in his infancy. He was born in the castle to Mary Queen of Scots and, legend has it, lowered in a basket so that he could be taken off and baptized in the Old Faith, a romantic story for which there is no hard evidence.

There is hard evidence enough, however, of the great siege of 1573. Scotland was rent by civil war, and one faction, the Confederate Lords, was backed by Queen Elizabeth. She sent ships loaded with troops and guns to Leith, just outside Edinburgh on the Forth, and we are told that five batteries bombarded the castle night and day. Though the principal tower, David's Tower, was partly destroyed and the well choked with rubble, the garrison grimly held on until the English took the outworks defending the eastern approach to the castle. The terms of surrender were agreed but were later violated: all the principal defenders were hanged at the Market Cross, their heads placed 'on the maist eminent places of the castell wall'.

Charles I spent the night before his Scottish coronation of 1633 in the castle. In 1640 war broke out again, two years before the Civil War began in England. The castle was held for the king but after a three month siege the garrison was starved into surrender.

After the end of the Civil War in England and the execution of Charles I, the Scots welcomed Charles II and proclaimed him at the Market Cross in Edinburgh, an act of defiance which

The entrance from the Esplanade, site of the annual military tattoo, with the Half-Moon Bastion behind.

provoked Cromwell to march north. He smashed the Royalists at the Battle of Dunbar on 3 September 1650, besieged the castle and was about to mine it after a three month siege when it surrendered. The governor, a Colonel Dundass, joined forces with Cromwell shortly afterwards, and there is fairly conclusive evidence that he did in fact betray the garrison.

Though the Civil War was the last time when most castles saw action, that was not so with Edinburgh. The English Bloodless Revolution which placed William III on the throne in place of James II in 1688 was not so easily accomplished in Scotland. There was a considerable rallying to the cause of James VII, as he was in Scotland. Another great three month siege took place before the forces of William III forced the Jacobite defenders into submission, just six weeks before the decisive battle of Killiecrankie when they won a famous victory but where their hero, Bonnie Dundee, was killed. Their cause died with him.

There was an unsuccessful attempt to seize the castle during the Jacobite Rising of 1715, but neither the castle nor the town fell. It was different in 1745. That year saw the last defence of the castle. It had been greatly strengthened by General Wade, the Hanoverian Commander who built so many splendid roads into the Highlands after the Rebellion of 1715 ('If you had seen these roads before they were made you would lift up your hands and bless General Wade'). So it was that when Charles Edward, the Young Pretender, entered Edinburgh in triumph at the head of his Highland army and took the city, the castle held out. During the six weeks that the Jacobites controlled the capital they could not take the castle, and from time to time the city suffered from its batteries.

This was the last time the castle saw any action. It served as a prison for many of those captured during the '45, and it was used as a prison too for successive batches of French prisoners during the wars against France in the second half of the eighteenth century and the Napoleonic Wars at the beginning of the nineteenth. No sovereign came here after Charles II until George IV made his great triumphant tartan-clad progress through Edinburgh in 1823. Since then most

Wilkie's portrait of George IV, the first sovereign to visit the castle since the reign of Charles II. Wearing the tartan, he processed through the city with great ceremony and style in 1823.

British sovereigns have also visited the castle, but they have always stayed at Holyrood House, where Charles Edward held his court in the '45. Today the castle, with its splendid museum and its many associations with the turbulent history of Scotland, is a tourist magnet but not a royal home. There is much to see here however (apart from the many exhibits in the Scottish United Services Museum) throughout the year. It still has a garrison, and every September it is the setting for the most splendid military tattoo in Britain.

The castle is approached along the great Esplanade, the nineteenth-century parade ground on which the tattoo is held. Part of this site was designated as Nova Scotia by Charles I, and it was on this symbolic tract of land that those who were made Baronets of Nova Scotia were given their nominal estates. A dry ditch, where once a drawbridge came down, leads to the castle entrance. There are few traces of the pre-sixteenth-century buildings anywhere. The massive Half-Moon Bastion has some detectable signs of David's Tower within it, revealed during the renovations at the beginning of this century, but the battery itself dates from the late sixteenth century, as does the portcullis. The principal buildings are grouped around Palace Yard in the south-east corner of the castle. Here we can see the room in which Mary Queen of Scots gave birth to James VI and I and the room where the Honours, or Crown Jewels, of Scotland are displayed. Here too is the early sixteenth-century great hall, with its hammer beam roof, one of the earliest in Scotland, and its splendid collection of arms and armour. Beneath the hall are the Casements, great vaulted chambers, some of which were used as prisons for the Jacobites and the French. To the west of Palace Yard and through the Foggy Gate are the Governor's House and the New Barracks built at the beginning and the end of the eighteenth century respectively.

One of the most famous features of the castle is not a building at all but a

The room in which Mary Queen of Scots gave birth on 19 June 1566 to the boy who became James VI of Scotland and James I of England – the first joint ruler of the two kingdoms. Over the fireplace hangs his portrait and on the ceiling are the royal crowned monograms. The coat of arms is that of the House of Stuart.

Mons Meg – the most famous cannon in Scotland. Made in the Low Countries in the fifteenth century, it was taken to England in 1754 but returned with great ceremony, escorted by three troops of cavalry and a pipe band, in 1829.

vast cannon. Mons Meg, which stands just outside St Margaret's Chapel, was one of the most massive pieces of artillery forged in the fifteenth century. The huge iron gun, over 4 metres (13 feet) long, could, when fully charged with 48 kilos (105 pounds) of powder, hurl an iron ball 1·5 kilometres (almost a mile), and a stone twice that distance. It burst when firing a salute in honour of James VII and II and this was reckoned by some to be an ill omen. It was taken to the Tower of London in 1754 but returned in great triumph in 1829, escorted from Leith by three troops of cavalry, the 73rd Regiment of Foot and a troop of pipers. Below Mons Meg is a small defence which has been used in recent years as a burial ground for dogs owned by soldiers of the garrison, a touching illustration of the fact that Edinburgh Castle has, again like the Tower of London, been a long inhabited citadel.

In the Scottish United Services Museum, which today occupies much of the castle, are many reminders of Scotland's past. Their presence helps to make the castle today what it has been since the Blessed Margaret died here, a focus of Scottish pride and patriotism.

The great hall, built at the beginning of the sixteenth century by King James IV. It is the finest of its period in Scotland, notable for its great roof, with carved human and animal masks at the base of the hammer beams.

# EILEAN DONAN CASTLE

## HIGHLANDS

THERE IS no more spectacularly sited castle than Eilean Donan, nor any castle in Scotland with a more fascinating history. It was the last British castle to see active service and was a heap of romantic rubble for two centuries until rebuilt, at vast expense and with great attention to authentic detail, half a century ago. The island of Donan, named after a saintly Celtic hermit who lived here in the early years of the seventh century, is at the head of Loch Duich and near to its confluence with Loch Long and Loch Alsh. The Picts were here before the Holy Man and visitors are shown vitrified rock as evidence of their fortification.

The island was refortified early in the thirteenth century by Alexander II against Norse and Danish invaders. In 1263 Alexander III gave it to Colin Fitzgerald for his services in the defeat of Haakon of Norway at the Battle of Largs, the battle which led to the Western Isles being ceded to Scotland.

Robert Bruce is said to have been given refuge here during his wanderings, and when he was king he sent his nephew, Randolph, Earl of Moray and Warden of Scotland, to subdue the rebels in the surrounding territory. We are told that fifty heads were displayed on the battlements of Eilean Donan as a warning to those who would challenge the royal authority. This was the territory of the

The island of Donan, a fortified site since the Picts were here, offered a strategic position from which to command the waters of Loch Duich, Loch Long and Loch Alsh. On the horizon are the Cuillin Hills of Skye.

McKenzies, Chiefs of Kintail, and in 1509 the castle was given to the MacRaes who formed their bodyguard and were known as 'McKenzie's Coat of Mail'.

The medieval Highlands were very rough country and the castle was involved in many raids and sieges, none so famous as the legendary siege of 1539 when Duncan MacRae held off a force of four hundred under Donald Gorme, a Lord of the Isles, killing the leader of the assailants with his final arrow.

It was almost two hundred years later, in 1719, that the castle saw its final action. The MacRaes were staunch supporters of the Jacobite cause and had taken part in the 1715 Rising. In 1719 there was another attempt – little known and rarely recalled – to place the Old Pretender on the throne. A small force of Spaniards was landed and they garrisoned the castle, but the Rising never stood a chance of success. The aid that had been promised from the

pristine glory in a dream and later to have found his vision verified by ancient plans stored in Edinburgh Castle.

Over the next twenty years, and at a cost of a quarter of a million pounds, Eilean Donan was meticulously restored in accordance with these plans. Today it again adds a special picturesque beauty to the road to the Isles, appearing, at a distance, as it would have done to Donald Gorme when he sought to invade it, or to the captain of *The Worcester* before he gave the order to fire.

The castle is approached from the loch over a stone arched causeway which leads to the forecourt of the main entrance. There is a portcullis in the outer walls and over it an inscription in Gaelic which reads, 'As long as there is a MacRae inside there will never be a Fraser outside'. The courtyard has all the appearance of an original medieval fortified settlement. Among the castle's most fascinating rooms is the Billeting Room with its 4-metre (14-foot) thick walls and barrel vaulted ceiling, much of it built by Farquhar MacRae, who also carved the extraordinary seven-headed Monster of Kintail from a piece of driftwood as a table centrepiece. On the walls are pictures of MacRaes dancing before the Battle of Sheriffmuir in 1715, and a print of the Battle of Glen

Continent did not come in sufficient numbers and on 10 May 1719 three of His Majesty's frigates, *The Worcester*, *The Enterprise* and *The Flamborough*, sailed up Loch Duich and in a matter of hours bombarded the garrison into submission and the castle into rubble.

PRECEDING PAGES Eilean Donan Castle on Loch Duich, from the east : the jewel on the road to the Isles.

It remained like this for almost another two centuries, one of the most popularly romantic ruins on the road to the Kyle of Lochalsh and the Isle of Skye.

In 1912 John MacRae determined to restore the home of his ancestors. Even in restoration the story of the castle is the stuff of legend, for one Farquhar MacRae was supposed to have seen the castle restored to its

FAR LEFT The courtyard, meticulously restored and rebuilt this century by John MacRae, descendant of the MacRaes who had supported the Jacobite cause in the 1719 Rising, when the castle was destroyed by English frigates.

LEFT James Francis Edward Stuart, the Old Pretender, for whom the castle fought and lost its final battle.

RIGHT The banqueting hall, with its fine collection of Sheraton and Chippendale furniture, family portraits and Jacobite relics.

BELOW The external walls of the Billeting Room are 4 metres (14 feet) thick and the barrel-vaulted ceiling 70 centimetres (2 feet 6 inches) thick at the centre. On the table is the 'Monster of Kintail'.

Shiel with which the 1719 Rising came to an end, barely a month after the destruction of the castle. There are other Jacobite relics and a set of cups used by Johnson and Boswell on their tour of 1773 – though they did not use them here : they approached Skye by another route.

In the banqueting hall, hung with portraits of the MacRaes, there are other relics from the third and final rebellion of 1745, when Prince Charlie raised his standard at Glen Finnan. There is also a wrought iron yett or gate from the earlier castle, which was recovered from the well during the restoration.

From the battlements there are magnificent views over the three lochs : to the right the entrance to Loch Long, to the left Loch Duich, and ahead Loch Alsh, stretching west to the hills of Skye. Family legend has it that the earlier MacRaes would toss their captives from the battlements. If they survived the rough waters they would be allowed their freedom. How true the story is we do not know, but they were rough times and it has a ring of truth, just as this magnificent reconstruction of a medieval Scottish fortress has an air of remarkable authenticity.

# 7 ROMANTIC

THE MIDDLE AGES cast a long and romantic afterglow. The squalor, the hardship and the brutality were quickly forgotten, and, seen through the eyes of poets and storytellers, the codes of conduct which we call chivalry attained an almost spiritual significance and exercised a strong influence over both the actions and the architecture of very different succeeding generations. If the knight was the perfect ideal of the Christian man of action, it was the castle that was his setting; attempts to relive his life inevitably led to attempts to recreate the authentic backcloth of his actions.

When the Wars of the Roses were still almost a living memory, Elizabeth's favourite, Leicester, entertained the Virgin Queen to a grand tournament in medieval style at Kenilworth. And elsewhere in the Midlands, at Woollaton in Nottinghamshire and at Bolsover (now a ruin) in Derbyshire, we can see Elizabethan and Jacobean houses that were greatly influenced by the medieval castle form.

# REVIVALS

The constitutional turmoil and civil upheaval of the seventeenth century brought a temporary halt to the recreation of scenes fit for chivalry. As we have seen, the castle came briefly into its own again. But as Commonwealth gave way to Restoration, stability returned, and the newly established men of wealth and power began once more to think of how they could best create great houses that would reflect their social position.

The new age of castle building began in earnest around the middle of the eighteenth century, when the Gothic fantasy once again took hold of the aristocratic imagination. The classical symmetry and simplicity of the great country houses of the first half of the century began to lose their attractions, and there was a new urge to build in a native style evocative of knightly virtues.

One of the earliest apostles of this new Gothic creed was the writer and dilettante Horace Walpole – son of Sir Robert Walpole, the earliest of our modern Prime Ministers. At Strawberry Hill he created a

turreted and pinnacled residence that was at once the delight and envy of his friends, many of whom were inspired to emulate his quaint architectural achievement. What better way could they do so than by crenellating their old houses, or by building new ones that would pass in the misty distance or the fading light as the homes of Arthurian figures ?

These eighteenth-century Gothic castles, built in an age of peace and plenty, contained within their towers and turrets, and hid behind their battlements, apartments of great comfort and splendour. One of the earliest of the totally new creations was Downton in Herefordshire. Here, on a splendid site overlooking the River Teme, Richard Payne Knight created a vast and comfortable mansion in the style of a castle, envisaging

FAR LEFT At Strawberry Hill (1753–78) Hugh Walpole created an exotic fantasy that was the prototype for a craze of Gothic extravaganzas.

LEFT The intricately decorated staircase at Strawberry Hill, its finials crowned with golden heraldic stags.

ABOVE Pugin, the greatest master of nineteenth-century Gothic architecture, designed the cathedral-like drawing room at Eastnor Castle just before he died. Heraldic devices cover the walls and fireplace, and the ceiling is hung with enormous brass chandeliers.

RIGHT Alnwick Castle on the banks of the Aln. Seat of the Percies since the fourteenth century, it was remodelled by Salvin in the nineteenth.

it as the crowning glory – as indeed it became – of the sort of romantic classical landscape that artists such as Claude and Poussin had painted in the seventeenth century. Knight saw the creation of a house in the diverse and irregular form of a castle as the perfect liberation from the constraints of classical architecture. He was one of the forerunners of the castle building boom of the early nineteenth century, of which the works of the partnership of Humphrey Repton and John Nash were such notable examples. One of the finest results of their collaboration was at Luscombe in Devon where they used military motifs to create a strikingly beautiful and unusual building.

Much more authentic and castle-like in appearance is Robert Smirke's Eastnor Castle in Herefordshire, built for the second Lord Summers and begun in 1812. This was meant to be a true replica of a medieval castle. It is said that Lord Summers spent £12,000 on bringing stones by pack mule from the Forest of Dean, although when it came to constructing the roof the shortage of timber caused by the building of warships known as 'England's wooden walls' (this was the climax of the Napoleonic Wars) led Smirke to improvise and use cast-iron stanchions instead of wooden ones for the roof trusses. The desire to play the baronial lord did not prevent the creation of a beautiful landscaped park with a magnificent ornamental lake, but it did persuade Lord Summers to bring in George Gilbert Scott to

design the great hall, an enormous room 18 metres (60 feet) long, 9 metres (30 feet) wide and 17 metres (55 feet) high, hung with a multitude of weapons and adorned with suits of armour. Eastnor was some forty years in the building and its famous drawing room is one of the last works of Augustus Welby Pugin, best remembered for his collaborations with Sir Charles Barry on the Palace of Westminster. Pugin was the most outstanding genius of all the Gothic architects of the nineteenth century. A prodigy, he designed furniture for Windsor Castle at the age of fifteen, was responsible for most of the interior of the new Houses of Parliament, and died, burnt out and mentally unhinged, at the age of forty in 1852. Most of his life was spent designing churches, and the Gothic drawing room at Eastnor has something of the atmosphere of a cathedral. Even the great brass chandeliers were based by Pugin on one from Nuremberg Cathedral that had been shown at the Great Exhibition of 1851.

Castle building and the cult of chivalry received an enormous boost from the novels of Sir Walter Scott. These inspired the so-called 'Norman' revival. Now it was not sufficient to have a Gothic castle : the ideal was to Normanize it as Thomas Hopper Normanized Penrhyn in North Wales for a Welsh slate millionaire. The cult of chivalry itself was elaborated in a remarkably influential book *The Broad Stone of Honour* by Sir Kenelm Digby, and saw its most famous dramatic expression in the extraordinary tournament staged by Lord Eglington at Eglington Castle on the west coast of Scotland in August 1839. There a hundred thousand gathered to see Lady Seymour preside as Queen of Beauty at a great medieval tournament. But the weather conspired against it and the whole thing was a fiasco.

There was something more of the noble than of the fiasco, however, about the bravely eccentric creation of Tennyson's grandfather, Charles Tennyson D'Eyncourt, who made for himself a setting of baronial splendour in the fastness of the Lincolnshire Wolds. There, in a hollow by the village of Tealby, he built Bayons Manor, a huge and elaborate replica of a medieval castle, complete with barbican, moat and drawbridge and a huge keep built as a ruin inside the inner wall. At Bayons this Lincolnshire squire entertained with enormous enthusiasm and extravagance. It was a remarkable place, and I well remember as a small boy clambering round the ruins and gazing in awe at the great hall and the antlers around its walls. Alas, Bayons is no more. Regarded as a dangerous structure, it was blown up in the mid-1960s.

Charles Tennyson D'Eyncourt used a local architect for Bayons, but the professional who advised him was perhaps the most skilful of all the recreators, Anthony Salvin. It was Salvin who built Peckforton in Cheshire and created a castle that could indeed have been defended ; and he was employed to re-authenticate the martial appearance of Rockingham in Northamptonshire, building there the 'ancient' tower in which Dickens, a friend of the family, wrote *Bleak House*. Salvin also supervised the restoration of Alnwick for the Duke of Northumberland and rebuilt Dunster in Somerset.

Other notable ancient castles that received the attentions of 'authentic restoration' were Powis near Welshpool, and Arundel, where the tenth Duke of Norfolk spent more than half a million pounds on Gothic transformations which the fifteenth duke demolished in his Normanizing programme a century later. Belvoir, the Leicestershire home of the Dukes of Rutland, built in the seventeenth century, was recreated in the Gothic style by James Wyatt at the beginning of the nineteenth century and rebuilt, after a disastrous fire, to the designs of the duke's chaplain in an earlier style twenty years later.

The most famous castle to receive the helping hand of a restorer was Windsor (of which more later), while possibly the most famous Gothic constructions of the nineteenth century are those which William Burges created for the third Marquess of Bute at Cardiff and at Castell Coch in Wales. Cardiff is as remarkable an extravaganza in its way as the Brighton Pavilion, and Castell Coch was almost a total recreation. North of the border, castles like Glamis and Dunrobin were extended and transformed, and there too extraordinary new castellated buildings were created, as at Inverary and Balmoral – the largest castle in Scotland and 'my darling Albert's own creation'.

# ARUNDEL CASTLE

## SUSSEX

ARUNDEL is best seen from the train as the railway line crosses the water meadows below this delightful Sussex town. Like Windsor from the motorway, it presents a stirring sight. And yet, as with Windsor, much of what we see from afar is the work of Victorian improvers, brought in by the fifteenth duke to 're-Normanize' his ancestral home.

But Arundel, again like Windsor, was one of the first of the Conqueror's strongholds. There are some splendid medieval remains here, and, beneath the work of the improvers, many further traces of the old castle.

There was a fortress here in Saxon times, and Arundel itself is one of the forty-nine castles mentioned in the *Domesday Book* in 1086. It sits on a chalk spur above the River Arun and just a few miles north of the Channel. Throughout the Middle Ages it was seen as a key link in the nation's defences against invasion. However, the three sieges suffered by Arundel were all the result of civil strife. The first came within a few years of the completion of the stone fortifications by Roger de Montgomery, on whom William the Conqueror had conferred the earldom of Arundel when he trusted him with command of part of the nation's coastal defences. In 1102 the castle passed to Roger de Belleme, Earl of Shrewsbury, a powerful but fickle nobleman who was one minute in favour with his sovereign, Henry I, and the next in league against him. He began to build the keep but the very same year he fell foul of the king, and held out in the castle for three months

The castle, high on its chalk spur above the River Arun.

against the Royalist force. After taking Arundel Henry I, and Henry II after him, continued work on the building, especially on the fine stone keep which commanded the castle from a 21-metre (70-foot) motte. Henry II added royal apartments and it was here too that Matilda took refuge when she attempted to seize the throne from her cousin Stephen during the civil wars of the 1140s. As a result Arundel saw its second siege as William d'Albini, who had achieved eminence by marrying the widow of Henry I, gave Matilda shelter.

Arundel is still held by descendants of d'Albini, though it has passed twice through the female line. first to the Fitzalans in the thirteenth century and then to the Howards, Dukes of Norfolk, in the sixteenth. It was Richard, first Earl of Arundel, who

An aerial view, showing the eleventh-century mound and bailey, the thirteenth-century barbican, and the extensive nineteenth-century additions.

built the upper part of the gatehouse and the two flanking barbican towers, and the fourth earl who a century later erected the glorious Fitzalan Chapel; restored in the nineteenth century, this is still the Roman Catholic family chapel of the Duke of Norfolk.

Because of their adherence to the Roman Catholic faith, the Howard family had a turbulent and disturbed history. Thomas, the third duke, was condemned to death and survived

ABOVE The magnificent Fitzalan Chapel, built in 1380 by Richard Fitzalan, first Earl of Arundel, and restored in 1886.

RIGHT Arundel from the south-east. Between the square twin towers are the lancet windows of the dining room.

only because Henry VIII died the day before the sentence was to be carried out. His son, Henry, was less successful in evading the scaffold in 1547 . He was beheaded nine days before the

death of the boy king, Edward VI. The Howards were safe during the reign of the Catholic Mary Tudor but two of them perished in the reign of Queen Elizabeth. In 1572 Henry's son was executed for plotting to marry Mary Queen of Scots, whose rosary we can still see in the castle. And that Howard's grandson, Philip, died in the Tower in 1595 after allegedly saying Mass for the success of the Armada and refusing to renounce his faith. His constancy was recognized. He was beatified after his death, and in 1970 he was canonized as St Philip Howard.

The Reformation meant that the parish church, of which the Fitzalan Chapel still forms a part, was separated from the duke's place of worship, an arrangement that persists to this day, though a fine Roman Catholic cathedral was built in the town by the fifteenth duke in the last century.

It was in the seventeenth century that Arundel saw its last siege : it was bombarded from the parish church in 1643 for nearly a month until the garrison surrendered. When the Cromwellians moved out in 1648 the castle was much slighted. After the Restoration Charles II restored the family to its lands and titles and made them hereditary Earl Marshals of England, a title they still hold, but little of the castle remained intact. It was not made even barely habitable until the middle of the eighteenth century, when Horace Walpole found it 'only a heap of ruins', with the Norfolks occupying a few 'cleapt up apartments' on their visits there.

Between 1791 and 1815, however, the tenth duke spent £600,000 in creating a great Gothic castle from the ruins, the masterpiece of the architect Francis Hiorne. We can still see the library he built in 1802, one of the finest early Gothic apartments in the country, renowned for the magnificence of its wood carving. Little else remains of the tenth duke's extensive attentions because between 1879 and 1910 the fifteenth duke set about

creating the great 'Norman' stronghold that we see there today.

The medieval remains are among the best preserved of any castle in Britain and although they consist only of the twelfth-century shell keep and main entrance, and the late thirteenth-century barbican, in themselves they justify a visit. Apart from these remains, and the curtain wall rebuilt in the 1850s, almost all that is now visible from the outside is the work of the 'improving' fifteenth duke. Having ensured that the keep

ABOVE The dining room, remodelled by Buckler in the Victorian Gothic style.

and barbican were carefully restored, he brought in the architect Buckler to redesign the whole castle.

His chapel is one of the finest examples of Victorian Gothic, particularly noted for its wonderful stained glass by Hardman, but the rest of the new Arundel is impressive not only for its splendid masonry and interiors but because of the many treasures it contains. Among the family portraits

ABOVE The sumptuous comfort and elegance of the late nineteenth-century drawing room – a dramatic contrast to its castellated exterior.

TOP The magnificent library, one of the few reminders of the first Gothic remodelling of the castle at the beginning of the nineteenth century : it was constructed by Jonathan Ritson in 1802. With its vaulted mahogany roof, it resembles a vast wooden model of a Gothic church.

are superb examples of the work of Daniel Mytens and Anthony Van Dyck. There is a magnificent armoury too, and fine furniture, much of it brought from Norfolk House, the palatial London home of the Howard family, which they were forced to give up to satisfy death duties in 1938. In satisfaction of further tax liabilities Arundel itself was handed over to a trust by the present duke in 1975, to be preserved for the nation.

For all its gracious furnishings and fine works of art, it is as a triumph of the romantic revival of castle building, set around some of the finest medieval remains in Britain, that Arundel is most worthy of a visit. It has the added advantage of being, like Ludlow, part of one of the least spoiled and most enjoyable of historic English towns.

# CASTELL COCH

## GLAMORGAN

CASTELL COCH was built in the thirteenth century to command the plain of Cardiff to the south and the narrow gorge of the Taff immediately below it to the west. Its site is a classic one – a natural stone platform on the steep slopes above the gorge, protected to the south and west by cliffs falling away to the valley, to the north by the slight depression separating the platform from the summit of the hill, and approached from the east by a path through beech woods.

In 1871 the ruins of the castle were uncovered by order of its owner, the third Marquess of Bute, who had succeeded to vast estates and riches in Scotland and South Wales in 1848. It was Bute's ambition to recreate, in elaborate and splendid medieval detail, his two castles of Cardiff and Castell Coch – or 'The Red Castle', so-called from the red sandstone on which it was originally built.

To achieve his ambition he commissioned William Burges. Work began at Cardiff in 1855 and in 1872 Burges presented his plans for Castell Coch. Work began here in 1875. The two great recreations are, together, the finest castles of the romantic revival. No other architect rivalled Burges's painstaking enthusiasm, meticulous attention to detail and consummate inventiveness. His work is worthy of comparison only with that of Charles Barry and of Pugin on the Palace of Westminster. Like the Palace, Castell Coch is an architectural masterpiece in its own right. It is no mere sham medieval fortress : it looks every inch a castle that could withstand attack.

Burges had the advantage of both a splendid and a virgin site, for there

Castell Coch's turreted skyline from the air, showing the Well Tower to the right, with its unroofed parapet, the Keep Tower in the centre, and the Kitchen Tower to the left. Linking the keep to the Kitchen Tower is the banqueting hall.

172

The main entrance to the castle, through the beech woods that surround it. To the left of the gatehouse is the Keep Tower, with the drawing room occupying the lower storeys and the lady's bedroom above. The drawbridge is narrower at the gatehouse end to create an illusion of greater length.

was almost nothing left of the old castle, destroyed in the fifteenth century and described as early as 1540 as 'al in ruine'. However, he followed the ground plan of the ruined castle with great accuracy while giving his own genius full rein in recreating the upper storeys.

Burges delighted in his fairytale site and created a turreted fairytale castle to match it. He insisted on conical roofs, seeking to prove that they were not only authentically medieval but authentically English as well, a point he did not successfully establish. Each of the three turret roofs, capping a great tower, is at a slightly different level and of a different shape. The tallest, on the tower south of the entrance, which Burges called the keep, protrudes slightly beyond the edge of its tower. On the other side of the entrance is a smaller and steeper cone within the battlemented top of the Well Tower, while the roof of the south-west Kitchen Tower is part cone and part pyramid. Together with tall chimneys, these turrets make an arrestingly picturesque skyline.

The dry moat is crossed by a wooden bridge. Originally Burges intended that the drawbridge and the portcullis behind it should be operated by a separate windlass, but Lord Bute, for all his medieval enthusiasm, jibbed at the idea of having a windlass in his bedroom, so both drawbridge and portcullis were operated by a single and simplified device. Moat, drawbridge and portcullis were not the only authentic defences Burges provided. He even went to the trouble of pointing out that the only entrance, across the moat and the wooden drawbridge, could quickly be sealed by firing the bridge. Outside the battlements of the Well Tower were a series of wooden flaps and horizontal hinges to protect the embrasures, a defensive feature he discovered in an illuminated manuscript in the British Museum. Burges wrote extensively about his design, explaining where each model came from and how every

defensive feature could be used.

The castle is surprisingly small. The courtyard is a mere 17 metres (55 feet) across, the three towers and three connecting sections forming an irregular ring round it. Moving clockwise from the entrance gate we come first to the Keep Tower, then to the hall, the Kitchen Tower, the curtain wall, the Well Tower and, finally, the gatehouse. That there is none of the rugged grandeur of the ruin here comes almost as a surprise after the authentic medieval appearance of the defences.

The interior of Castell Coch is not entirely the work of Burges. Unfortunately he died suddenly in 1881, long before it was completed, and his schemes had to be supervised by others, notably by William Frame, who had helped him at Cardiff. Nevertheless, what he called the Castellan rooms are a most remarkable triumph of the Victorian medieval imagination.

The drawing room, which occupies the full height of the first and second storeys of the circular keep, is covered with strikingly rich decoration. The panels covering the lower parts of the walls consist of fifty-eight vertical groups, each depicting a different plant. Above the doors are carved and painted mouldings derived from fifteenth-century manuscripts. On the west door are snails, lizards, caterpillars and butterflies; round the north-west door are mice and chaffinches,

and, round the south-west, birds'-nests with eggs and young. Decorating the main part of the walls are scenes from Aesop's Fables. On the over-mantle, carved figures represent the Three Fates from Greek mythology.

The banqueting hall, which is the first room you enter from the court-yard, measures 6 metres by 9 metres (20 feet by 30 feet) and stretches the whole distance between the Kitchen Tower and the keep. Here the dec-orations are rather more austere.

ABOVE LEFT A view across the courtyard, showing the covered wooden staircase leading to the banqueting hall.

ABOVE The two-storey drawing room in the Keep Tower, every inch of it covered with a wonderfully imaginative display of ornament. Over the fireplace are figures representing the Three Fates of Greek mythology – the daughters of Zeus and Themis who controlled the destinies of men. The figures below represent the Three Ages of Man.

OVERLEAF The lady's bedroom. Like the mouldings in the drawing room, the decoration on the capitals – a bird feeding its young, a kingfisher with a fish – derives from fifteenth-century manuscript illustration. But the real flavour of the room is determined by the use of gilt and mirrors, by arabesques on the painted wardrobe and by the extraordinary bed decorated with crystal balls. This pseudo-Moorish style emanated originally from a monumental work published in 1842 on the Alhambra Palace in Granada, which had greatly excited the Victorian desire for the exotic.

Neither here nor in the drawing room do we know who was responsible for the actual execution of the ornamentation and carving, though Burges left the most detailed drawings in his notebook.

The decorations in Lord Bute's bedroom rely mainly on stencilled geometrical patterns, similar to that of the banqueting hall. The lady's bedroom, which occupies the two top storeys of the keep, has an interesting double dome to make maximum use of the height of the conical turret. Attractive carved and painted capitals line the walls and fanciful oriental motifs decorate the bed and the wardrobe.

The castle consists only of these two major bedrooms, a drawing room, banqueting hall, servant's hall, kitchen and lavatories, but inside it is easy to forget the authenticity of military architecture after which Burges strove. His aim is immediately apparent, however, when we look outside, at the curtain wall and the Well Tower, where he endeavoured to reproduce faithfully the arrangements of the ancient castle he sought to recreate.

In his report before beginning work, Burges spoke to Lord Bute of his 'conjectural restoration'. He pointed out that, 'the knowledge of military architecture of the Middle Ages is a long way from being as advanced as the knowledge of either domestic or ecclesiastical architecture ... The restoration I have attempted will, I hope, be judged according to the measure of what is known and not what ought to be known.' A hundred years later we need not judge it by the standards set by architectural reproductions, but see it as a work of genius in its own right, perhaps the most outstandingly successful of all those romantic revival castles built for rich men desirous of indulging a fancy and reliving a dream.

The vaulted ceiling of the drawing room.

# WINDSOR CASTLE

## BERKSHIRE

WINDSOR IS the only royal castle that has been in continuous occupation since the Middle Ages and is the largest inhabited castle in the world. Almost every century from the twelfth to the nineteenth left its mark on this great fortress. It can be seen to best effect from the air: the sight of a stoutly defended citadel adapted to the opportunities and challenges of civilization can make the discomfort of using Heathrow airport positively worthwhile.

Windsor was one of the first sites chosen by William the Conqueror for the series of fortifications built to protect his new conquest after 1066. It was one of a ring of nine castles built by him around London, each some 32 kilometres (around 20 miles) from its neighbour and from the capital. William picked a superb site, a chalk outcrop rising sharply to 30·5 metres (100 feet) above the Thames and commanding splendid views over the countryside for miles around. On the mound, or motte, the tower keep was built; the bailey was longer and thinner than in most of William's fortresses to take full advantage of the castle's position. It was divided into three parts soon to become known, as they are today, as the upper, middle and lower wards. The moats were dry ones. To the south and west the lands were thickly wooded, for this was a royal chase and it was as a hunting lodge that Windsor was first used by the Norman kings.

The early castle was almost certainly built of wood, although it has recently been suggested that stone may have been used in the construction of the keep at the beginning of 1075. Certainly there are ample re-

cords of stone being taken from the quarries of Bedfordshire when Henry II built the spacious new royal apartments in the twelfth century. There are still visible traces of these apartments in the basement of the present ones.

Henry suffered, like so many medieval monarchs, from rebellious sons, and so had to turn his attention from improving the comforts of the castle to improving its defences. He began work on an outer wall with towers on the line of the original ramparts, and much of this still stands today around the upper ward. Even before they were completed, the new defences had to withstand the only two sieges in the castle's history. King John was responsible for both. The first came in 1194 when, as Prince John, he rebelled against his Crusader brother King Richard I while he was out of the country. Nobles loyal to the king besieged the castle but failed to take it. However, it was a hollow victory for John : his rebellion petered out and he surrendered to his mother's forces.

In 1215, after sealing Magna Carta at nearby Runnymede, John sought the Pope's absolution so that he could be released from the guaranteed rights which he had granted under duress to his barons. This was too much for the barons, and for three months they laid siege to Windsor. Again the castle withstood the siege but not before it had been extensively damaged.

This damage was repaired during the reign of Henry III who came to the throne a year later. He also enlarged Henry II's apartments. The next king to apply himself to extensive alteration at Windsor was Edward III (1327–77), who was born here and always held the castle in close affection. At Windsor he established his new order of chivalry – the Order of the Garter – making the castle chapel the chapel of the Order and creating a splendid timbered hall for the Garter ceremonies. A hundred years later Edward IV began to build what is still Windsor's crowning glory and one of the supreme achievements of medieval architecture, St George's Chapel. It was not completed until the reign of Henry VIII in 1528, when the beautiful fan-vaulted roof was finished.

Henry VIII was also responsible for the building of the main castle entrance, which bears his name. Under the terms of his will and in the reign of Queen Mary (1553–58) apartments

LEFT Windsor Castle : an aerial view of the largest castle in the world and the oldest continuously inhabited one. The foreground is dominated by St George's Chapel and the centre by the great Round Tower. The Queen's apartments are in the far right hand corner.

The massive keep restored by Wyatville.

were created for the 'Poor Knights', thirteen distinguished and elderly soldiers who, in suitable costume, would attend service on Sundays in place of the Knights of the Order. This they still do, though their successors were renamed the Military Knights by William IV in 1833.

The castle escaped siege or slight during the Civil War because it fell into Parliamentary hands at the beginning of the hostilities. Cromwell's forces treated the chapel with scant respect, using it as a store-house and stable, and, for a time, the castle served as a prison. Charles I himself was held there in his own former private apartments in the upper ward on two occasions, and after his execution in Whitehall in 1649 he was buried in St George's Chapel.

Following the Restoration in 1660, Charles II rebuilt the royal apartments, employing Grinling Gibbons to do the woodcarving and the Italian artist Verrio to paint the ceilings. He also planted the magnificent elm avenue, three miles long, to link the castle to Windsor Great Park.

Little more was done here until George III made minor alterations, replacing the classical windows of Charles II's apartments with Gothic ones. Windsor was George's favourite home. He spent much time there and was greatly loved by the local people,

ABOVE The Waterloo Chamber, designed by George IV's architect, Sir Jeffry Wyatville, to house portraits by Sir Thomas Lawrence of the sovereigns, statesmen and generals who had contributed to the downfall of Napoleon. The seamless carpet was made for Queen Victoria at Agra in India and is one of the largest in the world.

BELOW A watercolour of the castle c.1659, showing the keep in the centre and the domestic and royal quarters ranged around the quadrangle.

into whose homes he would often call without ceremony or announcement.

It was in the reign of George IV that the castle received its last major facelift and took on the appearance that we know today. Jeffry Wyatville was in charge of the works and the king took a strong personal interest in all that was done. He spent a million pounds on raising the round tower to make it the highest tower of any castle in the kingdom and on modernizing the royal apartments. It was a pro-

digious sum but one that time has justified, for little has been needed since in the way of major renovation or repair.

Because Windsor is still a principal royal residence, much of the castle is not open to the public and the state apartments themselves are not always on view. It is as well to check before making a visit. But no visit to Windsor is a disappointment. Unless there is a major service in progress, St George's Chapel is always open. It is a miracle of architectural grace. The roof of the nave, the west window, the choir stalls, the banners of the Garter Knights, are just some of its splendours. Henry VIII rests here and so does Jane Seymour, his favourite wife, and Edward IV lies in a superbly wrought tomb. More recently Edward VII and Queen Alexandra, George V and Queen Mary, and George VI were buried here. One of the saddest monuments is that to Princess Charlotte, only daughter of George IV, who died after the birth of a stillborn son in November 1817. Beneath the chapel (but not open to the public) is the royal tombhouse of George III, Queen Charlotte and six of their sons.

Other parts of the castle which a visitor should see are the Curfew Tower, with its sweeping view up the Thames towards Clewer and its hymn-

FAR LEFT St George's Chapel, Edward IV's great Chapel of the Order of the Garter, hung with the banners of the Garter Knights. At the far end of the magnificent fan-vaulted choir is the Sovereign's Stall.

LEFT The Queen's Guard Chamber, first used as such for Catherine of Braganza, Queen of Charles II. It now displays mementos of Britain's greatest admirals and generals, including Nelson, Marlborough and Wellington.

BELOW LEFT A small detail from the profusion of beautiful stonework in St George's Chapel.

playing bells, the lodgings of the Military Knights, and the Deanery where Sir Christopher Wren, whose father was Dean, spent his childhood.

The 'Norman Gateway' (which in fact dates from the fourteenth century) still has its portcullis above the outer arch. The gatehouse formed a state prison for John II of France and his son after their capture at Poitiers in 1356. They joined David II of Scotland, who had been taken at Neville's Cross ten years earlier. James I of Scotland was a prisoner here for eleven years from 1413 until 1424, and from here he watched the

beautiful Lady Joan Beaufort taking exercise in the garden at the foot of the round tower. He fell in love with her and married her.

Dominating the middle ward is the great round tower. The lower half dates from the twelfth century, but the tower that we see, a massive and splendid piece of apparent medieval fortification, is in fact the result of Wyatville's remarkably sensitive alterations at the beginning of the nineteenth century. The state apartments are themselves embellishments of Charles II's palace, and no one who has the opportunity to do so should miss the chance of seeing Salvin's great staircase, a triumphant attempt to build an imposing staircase within the confines of a fortress – or the Waterloo Chamber hung with Lawrence's portraits of the sovereigns, statesmen and generals who together brought about the downfall of Napoleon. All the state apartments are sumptuously furnished and contain some of the finest works of art in the royal collection, itself the greatest private collection in the world today. Its prize exhibits are the specially displayed Renaissance drawings, in-

cluding many by Leonardo da Vinci, and the portraits by Holbein of Henry VIII and his courtiers.

Windsor abounds in intriguing glimpses into our history. In the Queen's Guard Chamber are busts of Marlborough and Wellington beneath standards that are delivered to the castle each year by those great dukes' descendants as the 'rents' for the homes a grateful nation gave them for their victories. Marlborough's standard bears the arms of the kings of France as a reminder of his victories over the armies of Louis XIV, and it is sent to the castle on the anniversary of Blenheim, 13 August, as a rent for the honour and manor of Woodstock – where the first duke built Blenheim Palace. Wellington's standard is a tricolour to mark his victories against Napoleon and is delivered to the castle on 18 June – the anniversary of Waterloo – as the rent for Stratfield Saye in Hampshire. Both properties would revert to the crown if the rent were not paid.

There is more to see and delight in at Windsor than at any other royal house in Europe, and not only grand things evocative of great occasions. One of the most popular of Windsor's attractions is the enormous dolls' house designed by Lutyens for Queen Mary, to which many of the notable artists and authors of the day contributed tiny paintings, and books for the miniature royal library.

# OPENING HOURS

The publishers have made every effort to provide accurate information regarding opening times, but they sometimes change at short notice and it would be advisable to check with the property concerned before making a visit.

**MAIDEN CASTLE, Dorset**
*Department of the Environment*
Open, free of charge, during hours of daylight throughout the year.

**OLD SARUM, Wiltshire**
*Department of the Environment*
15 March–15 October Monday to Saturday 9.30–6.30, Sunday 2–6.30; 16 October–14 March Monday to Saturday 9.30–4, Sunday 2–4 (April–September inclusive open from 9.30 on Sundays). Closed 24, 25, 26 December, 1 January and 3 May.

**TINTAGEL CASTLE, Cornwall**
*Department of the Enviroment*
15 March–15 October Monday to Saturday 9.30–6.30, Sunday 2–6.30; 16 October–14 March Monday to Saturday 9.30–4, Sunday 2–4 (April–September inclusive open from 9.30 on Sundays). Closed 24, 25, 26 December, 1 January and 3 May.

**BERKELEY CASTLE, Gloucestershire**
*Mr and Mrs R.J.Berkeley*
April – daily (except Mondays) 2–5; May–August – weekdays (except Mondays) 11–5, Sundays 2–5; September – daily (except Mondays) 2–5; October – Sundays only 2–4.30. Grounds open until 6.

**DOVER CASTLE, Kent**
*Department of the Environment*
Keep and underground works: open all year. Castle: 15 March–15 October weekdays 9.30–6.30, Sundays 2–6.30; 16 October–14 March – weekdays 9.30–4, Sundays 2–4.

**LUDLOW CASTLE, Shropshire**
*Department of the Environment*
May–September – daily 10–6; November–April – daily (except Sundays) 10.30–4. Closed 24, 25, 26 December.

**ROCHESTER CASTLE, Kent**
*Department of the Environment*
May–September – daily 10–6; November–April – daily (except

Sundays) 10.30–4. Closed 24, 25, 26 December.

**TOWER OF LONDON, Greater London**
*Department of the Environment*
March–October – weekdays 9.30–5, Sundays 2–5; November–February – weekdays 9.30–4. Closed 24, 25, 26 December, 1 January, Good Friday and 3 May.

**CAERNARVON CASTLE, Gwynedd**
*Welsh Office*
15 March–15 October – Mondays to Saturdays 9.30–6.30, Sundays 2–6.30; 16 October–14 March – Mondays to Saturdays 9.30–4, Sundays 2–4. Closed 24, 25, 26 December, 1 January and 3 May.

**CAERPHILLY CASTLE, Mid-Glamorgan**
*Welsh Office*
15 March–15 October – Mondays to Saturdays 9.30–6.30, Sundays 2–6.30; 16 October–14 March – Mondays to Saturdays 9.30–4, Sundays 2–4. Closed 24, 25, 26 December, 1 January and 3 May.

**GOODRICH CASTLE, Herefordshire**
*Department of the Environment*
15 March–15 October – Mondays to Saturdays 9.30–6.30, Sundays 2–6.30; 16 October–14 March – Mondays to Saturdays 9.30–4, Sundays 2–4. Closed 24, 25, 26 December, 1 January and 3 May.

**KENILWORTH CASTLE, Warwickshire**
*Department of the Environment*
15 March–15 October – weekdays 9.30–6.30, Sundays 2–6.30; 16 October–14 March – weekdays 9.30–4, Sundays 2–4. Closed 24, 25, 26 December, 1 January and 3 May.

**BODIAM CASTLE, Sussex**
*National Trust*
1 April–31 October daily 10–7; 1 November–31 March – Mondays to Saturdays 10–Sunset. Closed 24, 25, 26 December.

**HEVER CASTLE, Kent**
4 April–31 October – daily (except Mondays and Thursdays) 11.30–6. Closed Good Friday.

**LEEDS CASTLE, Kent**
*Leeds Castle Foundation*
1 April–31 October – Tuesdays,

Wednesdays, Thursdays, Sundays and Bank Holiday Mondays (daily during July, August and September) 12–5; 1 November–31 March – Sundays 2–4.

**STOKESAY CASTLE, Shropshire**
*Sir Philip and Lady Magnus-Allcroft*
1 April–26 September – daily 10–6 (closed Mondays and Tuesdays in April, May, June and September; closed Tuesdays only in July and August); March and October – Wednesdays to Sundays 10–5.

**DEAL CASTLE, Kent**
*Department of the Environment*
15 March–15 October – weekdays 9.30–6.30, Sundays 2–6.30; 16 October–14 March – weekdays 9.30–4, Sundays 2–4. Closed 24, 25, 26 December, 1 January and 3 May.

**PENDENNIS CASTLE, Cornwall**
*Department of the Environment*
15 March–15 October – weekdays 9.30–6.30, Sundays 2–6.30; 16 October–14 March – weekdays 9.30–4, Sundays 2–4. Closed 24, 25, 26 December, 1 January and 3 May.

**RAGLAN CASTLE, Gwent**
*Welsh Office*
15 March–15 October – daily 9.30–6.30; 16 October–14 March – daily 9.30–4.30. Closed 24, 25, 26 December, 1 January and 3 May.

**CRATHES CASTLE, Grampian**
*National Trust for Scotland*
Castle: 9–12 April, 1 May–30 September Mondays to Saturdays 11–6, Sundays 2–6. Gardens: all year – daily 9.30–sunset.

**EDINBURGH CASTLE, Lothian**
*Crown Property*
May–October – weekdays 9.30–6, Sundays 11–6; November–April – weekdays 9.30–5, Sundays 12.30–4.15. Closed 25, 26 December, 1, 2 and 3 January.

**EILEAN DONAN CASTLE, Highlands**
*J.D.H.Macrae*
April–30 September – daily 10–12.30, 2–6.

**ARUNDEL CASTLE, Sussex**
*Arundel Castle Trustees Ltd*
1 April–29 October – daily (except Saturdays) 1–5 (12–5 during June, July and August, and all Bank Holidays).

**CASTELL COCH, South Glamorgan**
*Welsh Office*
15 March–15 October – daily 9.30–6.30;

16 October–14 March – weekdays 9.30–4, Sundays 2–4. Closed 24, 25, 26 December, 1 January and 3 May.

WINDSOR CASTLE, Berkshire
*Royal Residence*
Castle precincts: mid-March–30 April, 1

September–late October – daily 10–5.15; 1 May–31 August – daily 10–7.15; late October–mid-March – daily 10–4.15. Castle: late October–mid-March – weekdays 10.30–3; mid-March–late October – weekdays 10.30–5, Sundays

(early May–mid-October) 1.30–5. State Apartments: closed December, 1 January, mid-March–June; Queen Mary's Dolls' House: closed 25, 26 December, 1 January, 17 April and 18 June.

# OTHER CASTLES TO VISIT

## BEFORE THE NORMANS

BINDON HILL, Dorset
Fortified Iron Age site covering over 100 hectares (250 acres).

BLACKBURY CASTLE, Devonshire
Well preserved Iron Age hillfort on long, narrow ridge in open woodland.

CAERLEON-ON-USK, Gwent
Site of Roman legionary fortress. Defences can be traced but main attraction is Roman amphitheatre excavated 1926–8. Legend associates Caerleon with King Arthur.

HENGISTBURY HEAD, Hampshire
Fortified Iron Age trading base covering 70 hectares (170 acres).

HOD HILL, Dorset
Iron Age fort with outline of Roman fort within it.

HOUSESTEADS FORT, Northumberland
Most extensively excavated of the Roman forts on Hadrian's Wall.

PORCHESTER CASTLE, Hampshire
Roman fortress with wall almost complete. Built *c.* 300 AD; added to in Saxon and Norman times.

## THE NORMAN CASTLE

BAMBURGH CASTLE, Northumberland
Square three-storey keep. Curtain wall with D-plan wall towers. Barbican and outer gatehouse date from thirteenth century.

CASTLE ACRE, Norfolk
Square bailey. Foundations of large, square hall house converted into keep early in thirteenth century.

DURHAM CASTLE, Durham
High motte, triangular bailey and octagonal shell keep. Much altered and extended.

HEDINGHAM CASTLE, Essex
Five-storey keep in centre of ringwork.

LEWES CASTLE, Sussex
Oval bailey with motte at each end. One shell keep almost intact and remains of another. Twelfth-century wall towers.

LINCOLN CASTLE, Lincolnshire
Two mottes, one with shell keep and one with square tower.

RICHMOND CASTLE, Yorkshire
Triangular bailey and large square eleventh-century gatehouse.

ROCKINGHAM CASTLE, Northamptonshire
One of William the Conqueror's first castles, much altered in seventeenth and nineteenth centuries. Still occupied; fine interiors.

SHERBORNE CASTLE, Dorset
Rectangular bailey with early twelfth-century curtain wall and three square gatehouses.

YORK CASTLE, Yorkshire
Two motte-and-bailey castles on opposite sides of river; northern one has fine keep known as Clifford's Tower.

## THE CLIMAX OF CASTLE BUILDING

BEAUMARIS CASTLE, Gwynedd
Masterpiece of medieval fortification. Last of Edward I's great Welsh castles, built 1295–1330 and left unfinished.

CHEPSTOW CASTLE, Gwent
Norman castle extended and improved in thirteenth century, when second and third baileys, barbican and tower house added.

CHIRK CASTLE, Clwyd
Exterior is unique, unaltered example of Welsh border castle of Edward I's time. Contains fine furniture and decoration.

CONWAY CASTLE, Gwynedd
Fine example of Edwardian stronghold. Castle and town walls built as single scheme .

CRICCIETH CASTLE, Gwynedd
Dominates Cardigan Bay. Captured and extended by Edward I – English castle built within Welsh one, of which little remains.

FRAMLINGHAM CASTLE, Suffolk
Early example of castle without keep. Thirteen wall towers reminiscent of arrangement at Dover.

HARLECH CASTLE, Gwynedd
Another great Edwardian castle. Splendid clifftop site. Three baileys; concentric design.

KIDWELLY CASTLE, Dyfed
Unusual D-shaped plan based on earlier earthwork. Inner defences follow rectangular Edwardian pattern.

RHUDDLAN CASTLE, Clwyd
Remains of two castles: later, stone one begun end of thirteenth century – first concentric castle in Wales.

WARWICK CASTLE, Warwickshire
Most of existing castle dates from fourteenth century, but stands on Norman motte-and-bailey site. State rooms; superb collection of Old Masters. Park landscaped by Capability Brown.

## FORTIFIED MANOR HOUSES

CAISTER CASTLE, Norfolk
Built by Sir John Fastolf on model of German Rhineland castle. Brick with stone dressing.

COOLING CASTLE, Kent
House crenellated in 1381 to meet French invasion scare. Fine gatehouse.

HERSTMONCEUX CASTLE, Sussex
Well preserved courtyard castle built of brick in mid-fifteenth century. Interior much altered. Houses Royal Observatory.

NUNNEY CASTLE, Somerset
Begun in reign of Edward III. Fine rectangular tower house of Sir John Delamere, who served in French wars.

PENHURST PLACE, Kent
One of the finest of fourteenth-century manor houses. Magnificent great hall.

SCOTNEY CASTLE, Somerset
Fortified after French sackings of 1377. Picturesque remains of fourteenth-century castle with later additions.
TATTERSHALL CASTLE, Lincolnshire
Finest of brick keeps, faithfully restored by Lord Curzon.

## TUDORS AND STUARTS

BERWICK-UPON-TWEED, Northumberland
Finest set of artillery defences in England, built by Elizabeth I to defend town of Berwick against attack from Scots and their French allies.
DARTMOUTH CASTLE, Devonshire
Sixteenth-century artillery fort on site of earlier castle.
SOUTHSEA CASTLE, Hampshire
Designed by Henry VIII himself to guard Portsmouth Harbour. Houses interesting museum.
ST MAWES CASTLE, Cornwall
Well preserved artillery fort of Henry VIII's reign. With Pendennis, guards Falmouth Bay and Carrick Roads.
WALMER CASTLE, Kent
Henry VIII coastal blockhouse built as protection against invasion from Continent. Much altered; residence of Lord Warden of Cinque Ports.

## SCOTTISH CASTLES

BLAIR CASTLE, Tayside
Stronghold of Earls and Dukes of Atholl since thirteenth century; much altered in eighteenth century. Fine collections of china, lace, armour and Jacobite relics. Still headquarters of only remaining private army in U.K.

CAERLAVEROCK CASTLE, Dumfries & Galloway
Famous thirteenth-century Scottish castle of unusual triangular design. Pre-dates Edward I's great castles and fell to him in siege of 1300.
CAWDOR CASTLE, Highlands
Fourteenth-century tower house. Originally royal castle given to Thane of Cawdor in 1454. Rectangular plan dominated by central square tower.
CRAIGIEVAR CASTLE, Grampian
Romantic six-storey tower house of pink sandstone, built in seventeenth century and little altered since. Superb plasterwork ceilings.
DUNVEGAN CASTLE, Highlands
Continuously occupied by Chiefs of MacLeod since early thirteenth century. Much altered in nineteenth century. Houses famous Fairy Flag of Skye.
GLAMIS CASTLE, Tayside
Famous as birthplace of Queen Mother, and for associations with Macbeth. Originally royal hunting lodge; remodelled in seventeenth century in French château style.
STIRLING CASTLE, Central
Royal castle. Strongest of Scottish fortresses but changed hands more than any other.
TANTALLON CASTLE, East Lothian
One of first keep-gatehouses in Scotland, built in fourteenth century. Fine situation overlooking Firth of Forth.
THREAVE CASTLE, Dumfries & Galloway
Fourteenth-century tower house of third Earl of Douglas. Famous for Earl of Nithsdale's heroic defence for Charles II. Set in beautiful gardens on island in River Dee.

## ROMANTIC REVIVALS

BELVOIR CASTLE, Leicestershire
Seat of Dukes of Rutland since Henry VIII's time. Rebuilt by Wyatt 1816. Good furniture and pictures.
CARDIFF CASTLE, South Glamorgan
Most elaborate of recreations by William Burges for third Marquess of Bute. Wonderfully flamboyant interiors.
CULZEAN CASTLE, Strathclyde
Created by Robert Adam in 1780s around core of medieval castle on dramatic site above Firth of Clyde. Elegant classical interiors.
DOWNTON CASTLE, Hereford & Worcester
Rebuilt by Richard Payne Knight 1772–8 as focal point of classical landscape.
DUNROBIN CASTLE, Highlands
Medieval castle transformed 1844–50 into spectacular château for immensely rich second Duke of Sutherland.
EASTNOR CASTLE, Hereford & Worcester
Giles Gilbert Scott and Pugin produced some of their most impressive interiors for this early romantic revival built by Robert Smirke for Lord Somers.
INVERARAY CASTLE, Strathclyde
One of the earliest and finest of eighteenth-century Scottish Gothic revivals. Beautifully restored after disastrous fire in 1976.
PENRHYN CASTLE, Gwynedd
Splendid neo-Norman reconstruction for Welsh slate millionaire, begun 1827. Keep modelled on Rochester.
POWIS CASTLE, Powys
Home of Powis family for 500 years. Medieval castle restored 1900s. Fine interiors; magnificent terraced gardens.

# GLOSSARY

AISLE: The space between two arcades or between an arcade and an outer wall.
ARCADE: A row of arches supported by columns.
BAILEY: The courtyard of a castle and its surrounding buildings. Also known as a ward.

BARBICAN: An outwork from which the gateway or entrance to a castle was defended.
BARMKIN: The barbican of a pele tower or tower house.
BASTION: A projection of solid masonry, usually at the corner of a rampart.
BATTLEMENTS (or CRENELLATIONS): An indented parapet, made up of crenels and merlons.
BURGH: A fortified Anglo-Saxon township, generally on a hill.

CASTELLAN or CONSTABLE: The officer in charge of a castle.
CRENELLATE: To fortify. Hence crenel, a notch in a parapet.
CURTAIN: The connecting wall joining towers of a castle.
DONJON: The keep, or headquarters, of the lord of the castle.
DRAWBRIDGE: A movable bridge. Early drawbridges were moved horizontally like a gangway.
EMBRASURE: A small, usually splayed, opening in a parapet.

ENCEINTE: The circuit of walls and towers around a fortified stronghold.

FOREBUILDING: A building in front of a keep – generally containing the entrance to it.

FOSSE: A ditch.

GALLERY: A long passage or room.

GARDEROBE: Latrine.

HALL: The principal room in the keep, used for receiving guests and for major entertainments.

JOIST: The (normally wooden) wall-to-wall supports on which floorboards were fixed.

LANCET: A tall narrow, pointed window.

LOOP: A narrow opening for the discharge of missiles or arrows.

MACHICOLATION: An overhanging parapet on outer wall of castle, often over portcullis, with holes in its floor for dropping stones and missiles.

MANGONEL: Medieval siege engine for projecting stones.

MERLON: The solid part of an embattled parapet.

MEURTRIÈRES: Murder holes, for dropping stones on those below.

MOTTE: The artificial mound of earth on which the keep was generally erected.

MOTTE-AND-BAILEY: An earth mound with a wooden or stone keep surrounded by a ditch and fortified enclosure or courtyard.

ORATORY: A small private chapel.

PALISADE: A wooden defensive fence.

PARAPET: A low wall on the outer side of the main wall, protecting the front of the sentry walk.

PIER: A support for an arch.

PISCINA: A stone wash-basin set into or against a wall.

PORTCULLIS: A wooden or iron grille that slides vertically in grooves to block an entrance.

POSTERN: A (generally small) rear exit.

QUOIN: Dressed stone at the angle of a tower or wall.

RAMPART: The defensive wall or embankment surrounding a fort or town.

SHELL KEEP: A keep built in the form of a circular wall enclosing the motte top, or even the entire motte, and surrounding the castle's living quarters.

SLIGHT: To damage a castle in an attack.

SOLAR: The private living room of a castle, often over the hall and generally with a squint.

SQUINT: Observation hole in the wall of a solar, often into the hall below.

TREBUCHET: A siege engine.

WALL STAIR: A staircase built into a wall; when a spiral staircase, it is sometimes called a vice.

YETT: An iron gate – particularly in Scotland.

# ACKNOWLEDGMENTS

The publishers would like to thank the following for permission to reproduce illustrations and for kindly supplying photographs:

Aerofilms Ltd: 11, 18–19, 20–1, 24, 35, 40, 46, 62 left, 70, 80, 96, 102, 120, 128–9, 167, 180–1

John Bethell: 13, 32 right, 38–9, 48 bottom, 54 top, 66–7, 72 bottom, 75, 77 top, 81, 82–3, 85, 130–1, 132–3, 134, 136, 144–5, 160, 161, 165, 173, 175, 176–7, 178–9

Bibliotèque Nationale: 63

Bodleian Library: 118

J. and C. Bord: 14–15, 16, 20, 22–3, 23, 49 bottom, 53

British Library: 37 bottom, 45, 61 (Weidenfeld & Nicolson Archives)

British Museum: 182–3 bottom

British Tourist Authority: 49 top, 74–5, 162–3

By kind permission of the Duke of Buccleuch: 125 right (Weidenfeld & Nicolson Archives)

Peter Cheze-Brown: title page, 17 top, 25, 26–7, 28–9, 33 left and right, 46–7, 52, 62 right, 68–9, 76–7, 78 top and bottom, 79 top, 88, 90 top, 114–15,

116, 117 left and right, 119, 122, 126–7, 127 top and bottom, 131

By kind permission of the Master and Fellows of Corpus Christi College, Cambridge: 32 left (Weidenfeld & Nicolson Archives)

By kind permission of Viscount de l'Isle VC KG: 83 bottom

Department of the Environment: 42 bottom, 43, 54 bottom, 59 left, 65 top, 79 bottom, 121, 124 (Weidenfeld & Nicolson Archives)

J. Arthur Dixon Ltd: 159 top and bottom

England Scene: 42–3, 84–5, 103, 109, 110, 154–5

English Life Publications: 36–7, 38 top and bottom, 111, 112–13

Fotomas Index: 27

Robert Harding: 58 and 59 right (Weidenfeld & Nicolson Archives)

By gracious permission of Her Majesty the Queen: 150, 183 top, 185 top

By kind permission of Lord Astor of Hever: 98, 99 top

Lee Higham: 158 left

Michael Holford: 51, 64, 122–3, 182

Angelo Hornak: 104–5, 106, 106–7, 108–9

A. F. Kersting: 12, 41, 70–1, 72 3 top, 87,

100–1, 112, 115, 148–9, 156–7, 168–9

S. and O. Matthews: half-title, 92–3, 94 left, 166

National Portrait Gallery: 158 right

National Trust: 89, 94 right (photo John Bethell), 95 (photo Jim Stephens), 96–7 (photo John Bethell), 162

National Trust for Scotland: 138, 140 and 141 (Woodmansterne), 142, 142–3

Scottish Office: 151, 152, 152–3

B. and S. Shuel: 44–5, 55, 139, 174–5

Trans-Globe: 99 bottom, 101

Universitats Bibliothek Heidelberg: 83 top

Victoria and Albert Museum: 125 left (Weidenfeld & Nicolson Archives)

Wallace Collection: 48 top

Weidenfeld & Nicolson Archives: 90–1

Welsh Office: 172

By kind permission of the Dean and Canons of Windsor Castle: 185 bottom (photo George Spearman, Weidenfeld & Nicolson Archives)

Woodmansterne Ltd: 37 top (photo Jeremy Marks), 168, 170, 171 top and bottom, 184

The publishers would also like to thank the following for supplying artwork for reproduction:

Terry Allen Designs Ltd: 6, 34, 50, 56–7, 65, 77, 146–7

Alan Burton: 17, 31, 90, 137

191